PROBLEMS IN AMERICAN CIVILIZATION

THE POWER ELITE IN AMERICA

EDITED WITH AN INTRODUCTION BY

Norman L. Crockett

UNIVERSITY OF OKLAHOMA

D. C. HEATH AND COMPANY
Lexington, Massachusetts Toronto London

Printed in the United States of America

Library of Congress Number: 77–111480

CONTENTS

IV. THE MILITARY-INDUSTRIAL COMPLEX

INTRODUCTION

THE belief that a small, omnipotent group consistently conspires to formulate national policy lies deeply embedded in the American political tradition, but by the 1960's the nature of the power structure in the United States had become a question for open polemics —especially within the so-called New Left. Most present-day proponents of an elitist theory point to a number of important trends since World War II which have helped to create an atmosphere highly conducive to minority control. The constant fear of nuclear war on a global scale, coupled with huge government allocations for defense, has increased the power of the professional soldier in Washington, blurring the distinction between civilian and military authority. It is also suggested that the continued concentration of wealth through the formation of conglomerates cutting across industry lines, the resulting decline in the importance of small-scale enterprise, and the close cooperation between business and government in regulating the economy, appear to have heightened the influence of the corporate executive in politics. Perhaps most important, the inability or unwillingness of local, state, and federal governments to recognize and respond to major social problems, such as poverty, racial discrimination, and urban decay, and the ease with which powerful interest groups block legislation aimed at alleviating these ills, all lend credence to the charge that an "Establishment" dictates policy for the rest of the nation. Some Americans, especially the younger generation, exhibit a growing disenchantment with the status quo, and their complete rejection of traditional channels of communication reflects the demand that the system function according to its stated principles.

The average American faces a similar dilemma. Clinging to a deep faith in majority rule, yet confronted with a daily routine which seems increasingly dominated by impersonal forces beyond human control, many individuals experience difficulty in attempting to correlate democratic theory with everyday reality. The actions of others constantly impinge upon the movements of even the most powerful men and groups, and such constraints often lead to feelings of frustration. A myriad of factors, ranging from urbanization and the revolution in technology to the population explosion and the growth of bureaucracy, have tended to relegate the individual citizen to a seemingly minor role in the decision-making process. In turn, the security precautions arising from our heavy involvement in world affairs promote and multiply suspicions that the government occasionally manages news and hides behind a false veil of secrecy, ignoring the wishes of the people. And a few clever politicians, it is widely believed, compound the problem by capitalizing on the fears of the electorate during periods of crisis or uncertainty in an effort to gain public office or to enhance their own prestige. Thus, caught in the contradiction of a system that pays solemn allegiance to democratic rule, yet at every turn appears to reject that very principle, some individuals find it satisfying to believe that a hidden power elite rules America.

The readings in this volume have been chosen to examine the question of that power elite. Grouped into four major categories, the selections attempt to illustrate problems of conceptualization and method, as well as to reflect differences of opinion. The first group, containing six readings, focuses on definition and analysis in studying the nature of power in the United States. The two selections comprising group two examine social stratification and power, and those in group three are concerned with the corporate structure and power. The four selections in the final group of readings study the so-called military-industrial complex.

The first two selections, by sociologists C. Wright Mills and Floyd Hunter, constitute representative examples of the argument that America is governed by a small, monolithic elite. Mills' *The Power Elite,* published in 1956, enjoyed wide popularity and was heralded by many laymen as a thoughtful description of American politics based on clear evidence. Critics, on the other hand, attacked what they ironically called his Marxian assumption that all advanced industrial societies develop a ruling elite, and they further contended that the study distorted facts beyond recognition. Floyd Hunter's *Top Leadership, U.S.A.,* published three years later, essentially supported the Mills argument. Hunter utilized directories, registers, questionnaires, and a host of interviews with prominent individuals across the country in an effort to formulate a list of top leaders on the national level. In this selection, he discusses his methods and conclusions. Next appears a selection by Richard H. Rovere, a journalist and author of several books on politics. Rovere visualizes an "American Establishment," but unlike Mills and Hunter, he emphasizes influence rather than control. Its influence is pervasive in many areas, even though advertising, motion pictures, television, and both houses of Congress oppose the Establishment. Contrary to the findings of Hunter, Rovere argues that Establishment members possess only limited influence in state and local politics, primarily confining their activities to the national scene.

Leading the attack on the concept of a power elite is a selection from David Riesman's *The Lonely Crowd.* Riesman saw society composed of numerous veto groups, each formed around a common interest in order to check the actions of others, but together enjoying only brief consensus on a limited number of issues. Unity among groups proved quite ephemeral, evaporating with the solution of a particular problem. The fourth selection, from Arnold M. Rose's *The Power Structure,* brings the reader both the academic insights of a sociologist and the practical experience of a former state legislator. In the "multi-influence hypothesis," Rose envisions a number of elites, each attempting to formulate pol-

icy within its respective sphere of influence. Section one closes with an article by political scientist Robert A. Dahl. In "A Critique of the Ruling Elite Model," Dahl first argues that the proof of a power elite rests with those asserting the theory, proposes several possible tests for an elite hypothesis, and concludes that scholars have failed to examine the evidence necessary to substantiate the existence of such a group in the United States.

A portion of psychologist G. William Domhoff's *Who Rules America?* opens section two on social stratification and power. Domhoff analyzes a few of the problems inherent in attempting to delineate a "ruling class." The author then defends the "sociology-of-leadership" method, answers some of the critics of that approach, and closes with the assertion that the American upper class is indeed a governing class. Diametrically opposed to Domhoff is the next selection, from *Community Power and Political Theory,* by political scientist Nelson W. Polsby. Polsby systematically questions the use of "stratification theory" in the study of politics, contending that the assumptions and method directly lead the researcher to a predetermined conclusion.

Leaving the question of social stratification, section three turns to the corporate structure and power. The opening selection, by historian Gabriel Kolko, attacks the belief that the ownership and control of America's large corporations is widely separated and dispersed. Kolko maintains that a small group of business leaders hold the power necessary to manipulate the economy in any direction compatible with their own interests. However, in the next selection from *Power Without Property,* Adolf A. Berle, Jr., Professor Emeritus of Law, historically traces the changing relationship between ownership and power. To Berle, the ownership of American industry is rapidly passing into the hands of giant trust funds and foundations. Harvard economist John K. Galbraith continues the discussion with a selection taken from *The New Industrial State.* As a result of the growing necessity to coordinate action through systematic planning, and the tremendous advancements in technology in the past fifty years, power has shifted in American business enterprise from the individual to the group. The once powerful land owners, entrepreneurs, and holders of capital, have abdicated their positions to groups of highly skilled individuals, each member of the group being capable of providing specialized information relevant to a specific problem. A selection by political scientist Theodore J. Lowi concludes this section. Utilizing a lengthy review article as a springboard, Lowi analyzes a number of recent case studies of policy-making and then proposes a new framework for the study of power, incorporating the work of both the pluralists and the power-elite school.

The final section, dealing with the military-industrial complex, opens with portions of a speech by Senator Barry Goldwater. Goldwater chides liberals for their apparent obsession over the close cooperation between the active and retired military and the business community. Moreover, he praises both industry and the military for providing a protective shield for the nation. Shifting the emphasis, sociologist Irving L. Horowitz directs the reader's attention to the "new civilian militarists," in an excerpt from *The War Game*. According to Horowitz, the real danger lies not with the defense department, corporate leaders, or over zealous joint-chiefs-of-staff, but with civilian advisors who formulate military policy without considering the moral implications of their advice. In the following selection, Morris Janowitz, sociologist and recognized authority on the military personality, questions the idea that professional soldiers constitute an important segment of a power elite. On the contrary, Janowitz believes that the background, interests, and training of the career officer, along with

his social isolation, eliminate the possibility of close cooperation with the civilian community. Marc Pilisuk and Thomas Hayden conclude section four, and the volume, with the question, "Is There A Military-Industrial Complex Which Prevents Peace?" Focusing attention on the "core beliefs" which tend to influence actions at home and abroad, the two authors contend that it no longer remains a simple question of minority control by a small coalition composed of business executives and generals. Indeed, the American values system makes the entire country a giant military-industrial complex.

As the reader begins each section, a few basic questions might help to clarify the discussion. Does the discipline or profession of the author (economics, psychology, sociology, . . .) tend to shape his conception of the problem? With what assumptions and frame of reference does each writer appear to begin? Do some assume the existence of a power elite and argue from that point? Or, on the other hand, does the author automatically rule out the existence of such a group and focus attention on other aspects of the question? On what type of evidence does the argument appear to be based? Is the author concerned with the use or abuse of power (which may involve a value judgement) or its structure? From the approach, can one hypothesize about the political philosophy of the author? And finally, to prove or disprove the existence of a power elite in America, what questions must be raised and answered? Disagreement often promotes further inquiry, and hopefully the reading selections have generated additional ideas encouraging more reading and research, for in the major proposition under consideration, the nature and extent of power, lies the future of the American system.

CONFLICT OF OPINION

On the Power Elite:

... the political directorate, the corporate rich, and the ascendant military have come together as the power elite, and the expanded and centralized hierarchies which they head have encroached upon the old balances and have now relegated them to the middle levels of power.

—C. WRIGHT MILLS

For ourselves, we conclude that the income, wealth, and institutional leadership of what Baltzell calls the "American business aristocracy" are more than sufficient to earn it the designation "governing class." As Sweezy would say, this "ruling class" is based upon the national corporate economy and the institutions that economy nourishes. It manifests itself through what the late C. Wright Mills called the power elite.

—G. WILLIAM DOMHOFF

The only leaders of national scope left in the United States today are those who can placate the veto groups. The only followers left in the United States today are those unorganized and sometimes disorganized unfortunates who have not yet invented their group.

—DAVID RIESMAN

... the evidence for a ruling elite, either in the United States or in any specific community, has not yet been properly examined so far as I know.

—ROBERT A. DAHL

On Corporate Power:

The real questions are: (1) Do a small group of very wealthy men have the power to guide industry, and thereby much of the total economy, toward ends that they decide upon as compatible with their own interests? (2) Do they own and control the major corporations? The answers must inevitably be affirmative.

—GABRIEL KOLKO

Power has, in fact, passed to what anyone in search of novelty might be justified in calling a new factor of production. This is the association of men of diverse technical knowledge, experience or other talent which modern industrial technology and planning require.

—JOHN K. GALBRAITH

On the Military-Industrial Complex:

There is little evidence to support the argument that the military forms an integral part of a compact social group which constitutes the power elite. Rather, in fact, the contrary seems to be the case: namely, the political behavior of the military in the United States is still deeply conditioned by its social isolation.

—MORRIS JANOWITZ

Is there, then, a military-industrial complex which prevents peace? The answer is inextricably imbedded into the mainstream of American institutions and mores. ... Our concept is more clearly that American society *is* a military-industrial complex.

—MARC PILISUK AND THOMAS HAYDEN

I. THE AMERICAN POWER STRUCTURE: PROBLEMS OF DEFINITION AND ANALYSIS

C. Wright Mills

THE HIGHER CIRCLES

Only a few books published in the twentieth century have generated more intellectual curiosity than C. Wright Mills' *The Power Elite*. Within a short time a host of scholars, representing all disciplines of the social sciences, had launched investigations purporting to test the basic hypothesis that a small cadre of corporate, military, and political leaders ruled the United States. In the following excerpt from that study, Mills examines the structure of power in America.

THE powers of ordinary men are circumscribed by the everyday worlds in which they live, yet even in these rounds of job, family, and neighborhood they often seem driven by forces they can neither understand nor govern. 'Great changes' are beyond their control, but affect their conduct and outlook none the less. The very framework of modern society confines them to projects not their own, but from every side, such changes now press upon the men and women of the mass society, who accordingly feel that they are without purpose in an epoch in which they are without power.

But not all men are in this sense ordinary. As the means of information and of power are centralized, some men come to occupy positions in American society from which they can look down upon, so to speak, and by their decisions mightily affect, the everyday worlds of ordinary men and women. They are not made by their jobs; they set up and break down jobs for thousands of others; they are not confined by simple family responsibilities; they can escape. They may live in many hotels and houses, but they are bound by no one community. They need not merely 'meet the demands of the day and hour'; in some part, they create these demands, and cause others to meet them. Whether or not they profess their power, their technical and political experience of it far transcends that of the underlying population. What Jacob Burckhardt said of 'great men,' most Americans might well say of their elite: 'They are all that we are not.'[1]

The power elite is composed of men whose positions enable them to transcend the ordinary environments of ordinary men and women; they are in positions to make decisions having major consequences. Whether they do or do not make such decisions is less important than the fact that they do occupy such pivotal positions: their failure to act, their failure to make decisions, is itself an act that is often of greater consequence than the decisions they do make. For they are in command of the major hierarchies and organizations of modern society. They rule the big corporations.

[1] Jacob Burckhardt, *Force and Freedom*, New York, 1943, 308ff.

They run the machinery of the state and claim its prerogatives. They direct the military establishment. They occupy the strategic command posts of the social structure, in which are now centered the effective means of the power and the wealth and the celebrity which they enjoy.

The power elite are not solitary rulers. Advisers and consultants, spokesmen and opinion-makers are often the captains of their higher thought and decision. Immediately below the elite are the professional politicians of the middle levels of power, in the Congress and in the pressure groups, as well as among the new and old upper classes of town and city and region. Mingling with them . . . are those professional celebrities who live by being continually displayed but are never, so long as they remain celebrities, displayed enough. If such celebrities are not at the head of any dominating hierarchy, they do often have the power to distract the attention of the public or afford sensations to the masses, or, more directly, to gain the ear of those who do occupy positions of direct power. More or less unattached, as critics of morality and technicians of power, as spokesmen of God and creators of mass sensibility, such celebrities and consultants are part of the immediate scene in which the drama of the elite is enacted. But that drama itself is centered in the command posts of the major institutional hierarchies.

The truth about the nature and the power of the elite is not some secret which men of affairs know but will not tell. Such men hold quite various theories about their own roles in the sequence of event and decision. Often they are uncertain about their roles, and even more often they allow their fears and their hopes to affect their assessment of their own power. No matter how great their actual power, they tend to be less acutely aware of it than of the resistances of others to its use. Moreover, most American men of affairs have learned well the rhetoric of public relations, in some cases even to the point of using it when they are alone, and thus coming to believe it. The personal awareness of the

actors is only one of the several sources one must examine in order to understand the higher circles. Yet many who believe that there is no elite, or at any rate none of any consequence, rest their argument upon what men of affairs believe about themselves, or at least assert in public.

There is, however, another view: those who feel, even if vaguely, that a compact and powerful elite of great importance does now prevail in America often base that feeling upon the historical trend of our time. They have felt, for example, the domination of the military event, and from this they infer that generals and admirals, as well as other men of decision influenced by them, must be enormously powerful. They hear that the Congress has again abdicated to a handful of men decisions clearly related to the issue of war or peace. They know that the bomb was dropped over Japan in the name of the United States of America, although they were at no time consulted about the matter. They feel that they live in a time of big decisions; they know that they are not making any. Accordingly, as they consider the present as history, they infer that at its center, making decisions or failing to make them, there must be an elite of power.

On the one hand, those who share this feeling about big historical events assume that there is an elite and that its power is great. On the other hand, those who listen carefully to the reports of men apparently involved in the great decisions often do not believe that there is an elite whose powers are of decisive consequence.

Both views must be taken into account, but neither is adequate. The way to understand the power of the American elite lies neither solely in recognizing the historic scale of events nor in accepting the personal awareness reported by men of apparent decision. Behind such men and behind the events of history, linking the two, are the major institutions of modern society. These hierarchies of state and corporation and army constitute the means of power; as such they are now of a consequence not before equaled in human history—and at their summits, there are now those command posts of modern society which offer us the sociological key to an understanding of the role of the higher circles in America.

Within American society, major national power now resides in the economic, the political, and the military domains. Other institutions seem off to the side of modern history, and, on occasion, duly subordinated to these. No family is as directly powerful in national affairs as any major corporation; no church is as directly powerful in the external biographies of young men in America today as the military establishment; no college is as powerful in the shaping of momentous events as the National Security Council. Religious, educational, and family institutions are not autonomous centers of national power; on the contrary, these decentralized areas are increasingly shaped by the big three, in which developments of decisive and immediate consequence now occur.

Families and churches and schools adapt to modern life; governments and armies and corporations shape it; and, as they do so, they turn these lesser institutions into means for their ends. Religious institutions provide chaplains to the armed forces where they are used as a means of increasing the effectiveness of its morale to kill. Schools select and train men for their jobs in corporations and their specialized tasks in the armed forces. The extended family has, of course, long been broken up by the industrial revolution, and now the son and the father are removed from the family, by compulsion if need be, whenever the army of the state sends out the call. And the symbols of all these lesser institutions are used to legitimate the power and the decisions of the big three.

The life-fate of the modern individual depends not only upon the family into which he was born or which he enters by marriage, but increasingly upon the corporation in which he spends the most alert hours of his best years; not only upon the school where he is educated as a child and adolescent, but also upon the state which touches him throughout his life; not only upon the church in which on occasion he hears the word of God, but also upon the army in which he is disciplined.

If the centralized state could not rely upon the inculcation of nationalist loyalties in public and private schools, its leaders would promptly seek to modify the decentralized educational system. If the bankruptcy rate among the top five hundred corporations were as high as the general divorce rate among the thirty-seven million married couples, there would be economic catastrophe on an international scale. If members of armies gave to them no more of their lives than do believers to the churches to which they belong, there would be a military crisis.

Within each of the big three, the typical institutional unit has become enlarged, has become administrative, and, in the power of its decisions, has become centralized. Behind these developments there is a fabulous technology, for as institutions, they have incorporated this technology and guide it, even as it shapes and paces their developments.

The economy—once a great scatter of small productive units in autonomous balance—has become dominated by two or three hundred giant corporations, administratively and politically interrelated, which together hold the keys to economic decisions.

The political order, once a decentralized set of several dozen states with a weak spinal cord, has become a centralized, executive establishment which has taken up into itself many powers previously scattered, and now enters into each and every cranny of the social structure.

The military order, once a slim establishment in a context of distrust fed by state militia, has become the largest and most expensive feature of government, and, although well versed in smiling public relations, now has all the grim and clumsy efficiency of a sprawling bureaucratic domain.

In each of these institutional areas, the means of power at the disposal of decision makers have increased enormously; their central executive powers have been enhanced; within each of them modern administrative routines have been elaborated and tightened up.

As each of these domains becomes enlarged and centralized, the consequences of its activities become greater, and its traffic with the others increases. The decisions of a handful of corporations bear upon military and political as well as upon economic developments around the world. The decisions of the military establishment rest upon and grievously affect political life as well as the very level of economic activity. The decisions made within the political domain determine economic activities and military programs. There is no longer, on the one hand, an economy, and, on the other hand, a political order containing a military establishment unimportant to politics and to money-making. There is a political economy linked, in a thousand ways, with military institutions and decisions. On each side of the world-split running through central Europe and around the Asiatic rimlands, there is an ever-increasing interlocking of economic, military, and political structures. If there is government intervention in the corporate economy, so is there corporate intervention in the governmental process. In the structural sense, this triangle of power is the source of the interlocking directorate that is most important for the historical structure of the present.

The fact of the interlocking is clearly revealed at each of the points of crisis of modern capitalist society—slump, war, and boom. In each, men of decision are led to an awareness of the interdependence of the major institutional orders. In the nineteenth century, when the scale of all institutions was smaller, their liberal integration was achieved in the automatic economy, by an autonomous play of market forces, and in the automatic political domain, by the bargain and the vote. It was then assumed that out of the imbalance and friction that followed the limited decisions then possible a new equilibrium would in due course emerge. That can no longer be assumed, and it is not assumed by the men at the top of each of the three dominant hierarchies.

For given the scope of their consequences, decisions—and indecisions—in any one of these ramify into the others, and hence top decisions tend either to become co-ordinated or to lead to a commanding indecision. It has not always been like this. When numerous small entrepreneurs made up the economy, for example, many of them could fail and the consequences still remain local; political and military authorities did not intervene. But now, given political expectations and military commitments, can they afford to allow key units of the private corporate economy to break down in slump? Increasingly, they do intervene in economic affairs, and as they do so, the controlling decisions in each order are inspected by agents of the other two, and economic, military, and political structures are interlocked.

At the pinnacle of each of the three enlarged and centralized domains, there have arisen those higher circles which make up the economic, the political, and the military elites. At the top of the economy, among the corporate rich, there are the chief executives; at the top of the political order, the members of the political directorate; at the top of the military establishment, the elite of soldier-statesmen clustered in and around the Joint Chiefs of Staff and the upper echelon. As each of these domains has coincided with the others, as decisions tend to become total in their consequence, the leading men in each of the three domains of power—the warlords, the corporation chieftains, the political directorate—tend to come together, to form the power elite of America.

*   *   *

Such an elite may be conceived as omnipotent, and its powers thought of as a great hidden design. Thus, in vulgar Marxism, events and trends are explained by reference to 'the will of the bourgeoisie'; in Nazism, by reference to 'the conspiracy of the Jews'; by the petty right in America today, by reference to 'the hidden force' of Communist spies. According to such notions of the omnipotent elite as historical cause, the elite is never an entirely visible agency. It is, in fact, a secular substitute for the will of God, being realized in a sort of providential design, except that usually non-elite men are thought capable of opposing it and eventually overcoming it.

The opposite view—of the elite as impotent—is now quite popular among liberal-minded observers. Far from being omnipotent, the elites are thought to be so scattered as to lack any coherence as a historical force. Their invisibility is not the invisibility of secrecy but the invisibility of the multitude. Those who occupy the formal places of authority are so check-mated—by other elites exerting pressure, or by the public as an electorate, or by constitutional codes—that, although there may be upper classes, there is no ruling class; although there may be men of power, there is no power elite; although there may be a system of stratification, it has no effective top. In the extreme, this view of the elite, as weakened by compromise and disunited to the point of nullity, is a substitute for impersonal collective fate; for, in this view, the decisions of the visible men of the higher circles do not count in history.

Internationally, the image of the omnipotent elite tends to prevail. All good events and pleasing happenings are quickly imputed by the opinion-makers to the leaders of their own nation; all bad events and unpleasant experiences are imputed to the enemy abroad. In both cases, the omnipotence of evil rulers or of virtuous leaders is assumed. Within the nation, the use of such rhetoric is rather more complicated: when men speak of the power of their own party or circle, they and their leaders are, of course, impotent; only 'the people' are omnipotent. But, when they speak of the power of their opponent's party or circle, they impute to them omnipotence; 'the people' are now powerlessly taken in.

More generally, American men of power tend, by convention, to deny that they are powerful. No American runs for office in order to rule or even govern, but only to serve; he does not become a bureaucrat or even an official, but a public servant. And nowadays, as I have al-ready pointed out, such postures have become standard features of the public-relations programs of all men of power. So firm a part of the style of power-wielding have they become that conservative writers readily misinterpret them as indicating a trend toward an 'amorphous power situation.'

But the 'power situation' of America today is less amorphous than is the perspective of those who see it as a romantic confusion. It is less a flat, momentary 'situation' than a graded, durable structure. And if those who occupy its top grades are not omnipotent, neither are they impotent. It is the form and the height of the gradation of power that we must examine if we would understand the degree of power held and exercised by the elite.

If the power to decide such national issues as are decided were shared in an absolutely equal way, there would be no power elite; in fact, there would be no *gradation* of power, but only a radical homogeneity. At the opposite extreme as well, if the power to decide issues were absolutely monopolized by one small group, there would be no gradation of power; there would simply be this small group in command, and below it, the undifferentiated, dominated masses. American society today represents neither the one nor the other of these extremes, but a conception of them is none the less useful: it makes us realize more clearly the question of the structure of power in the United States and the position of the power elite within it.

Within each of the most powerful institutional orders of modern society there is a gradation of power. The owner of a roadside fruit stand does not have as much power in any area of social or economic or political decision as the head of a multi-million-dollar fruit corporation; no lieutenant on the line is as powerful as the Chief of Staff in the Pentagon; no deputy sheriff carries as much authority as the President of the United States. Accordingly, the problem of defining the power elite concerns the level at which we wish to draw the line. By lowering the line, we could define the elite out of existence; by raising it, we

under pretence of a public servant.

could make the elite a very small circle indeed. In a preliminary and minimum way, we draw the line crudely, in charcoal as it were: By the power elite, we refer to those political, economic, and military circles which as an intricate set of overlapping cliques share decisions having at least national consequences. In so far as national events are decided, the power elite are those who decide them.

To say that there are obvious gradations of power and of opportunities to decide within modern society is not to say that the powerful are united, that they fully know what they do, or that they are consciously joined in conspiracy. Such issues are best faced if we concern ourselves, in the first instance, more with the structural position of the high and mighty, and with the consequences of their decisions, than with the extent of their awareness or the purity of their motives. To understand the power elite, we must attend to three major keys:

I. One, which we shall emphasize throughout our discussion of each of the higher circles, is the psychology of the several elites in their respective milieux. In so far as the power elite is composed of men of similar origin and education, in so far as their careers and their styles of life are similar, there are psychological and social bases for their unity, resting upon the fact that they are of similar social type and leading to the fact of their easy intermingling. This kind of unity reaches its frothier apex in the sharing of that prestige that is to be had in the world of the celebrity; it achieves a more solid culmination in the fact of the interchangeability of positions within and between the three dominant institutional orders.

II. Behind such psychological and social unity as we may find, are the structure and the mechanics of those institutional hierarchies over which the political directorate, the corporate rich, and the high military now preside. The greater the scale of these bureaucratic domains, the greater the scope of their respective elite's power. How each of the major hierarchies is shaped and what relations it has with the other hierarchies determine in large part the relations of their rulers. If these hierarchies are scattered and disjointed, then their respective elites tend to be scattered and disjointed; if they have many interconnections and points of coinciding interest, then their elites tend to form a coherent kind of grouping.

The unity of the elite is not a simple reflection of the unity of institutions, but men and institutions are always related, and our conception of the power elite invites us to determine that relation. Today in America there are several important structural coincidences of interest between these institutional domains, including the development of a permanent war establishment by a privately incorporated economy inside a political vacuum.

III. The unity of the power elite, however, does not rest solely on psychological similarity and social intermingling, nor entirely on the structural coincidences of commanding positions and interests. At times it is the unity of a more explicit co-ordination. To say that these three higher circles are increasingly co-ordinated, that this is *one* basis of their unity, and that at times—as during the wars—such co-ordination is quite decisive, is not to say that the co-ordination is total or continuous, or even that it is very surefooted. Much less is it to say that willful co-ordination is the sole or the major basis of their unity, or that the power elite has emerged as the realization of a plan. But it is to say that as the institutional mechanics of our time have opened up avenues to men pursuing their several interests, many of them have come to see that these several interests could be realized more easily if they worked together, in informal as well as in more formal ways, and accordingly they have done so.

*   *   *

We study history, it has been said, to rid ourselves of it, and the history of the power elite is a clear case for which this maxim is correct. Like the tempo of American life in general, the long-term trends of the power structure have been greatly speeded up since World War II, and certain newer trends within and between the dominant institutions have also set the shape of the power elite and given historically specific meaning to its fifth epoch:

I. In so far as the structural clue to the power elite today lies in the political order, that clue is the decline of politics as genuine and public debate of alternative decisions—with nationally responsible and policy-coherent parties and with autonomous organizations connecting the lower and middle levels of power with the top levels of decision. America is now in considerable part more a formal political democracy than a democratic social structure, and even the formal political mechanics are weak.

The long-time tendency of business and government to become more intricately and deeply involved with each other has, in the fifth epoch, reached a new point of explicitness. The two cannot now be seen clearly as two distinct worlds. It is in terms of the executive agencies of the state that the rapprochement has proceeded most decisively. The growth of the executive branch of the government, with its agencies that patrol the complex economy, does not mean merely the 'enlargement of government' as some sort of autonomous bureaucracy: it has meant the ascendancy of the corporation's man as a political eminence.

During the New Deal the corporate chieftains joined the political directorate; as of World War II they have come to dominate it. Long interlocked with government, now they have moved into quite full direction of the economy of the war effort and of the postwar era. This shift of the corporation executives into the political directorate has accelerated the long-term relegation of the professional politicians in the Congress to the middle levels of power.

II. In so far as the structural clue to the power elite today lies in the enlarged and military state, that clue becomes evident in the military ascendancy. The warlords have gained decisive political relevance, and the military structure of America is now in considerable part a political structure. The seemingly permanent military threat places a premium on the military and upon their control of men, materiel, money, and power; virtually all political and economic actions are now judged in terms of military definitions of reality: the higher warlords have ascended to a firm position within the power elite of the fifth epoch.

In part at least this has resulted from one simple historical fact, pivotal for the years since 1939: the focus of elite attention has been shifted from domestic problems, centered in the 'thirties around slump, to international problems, centered in the 'forties and 'fifties around war. Since the governing apparatus of the United States has by long historic usage been adapted to and shaped by domestic clash and balance, it has not, from any angle, had suitable agencies and traditions for the handling of international problems. Such formal democratic mechanics as had arisen in the century and a half of national development prior to 1941, had not been extended to the American handling of international affairs. It is, in considerable part, in this vacuum that the power elite has grown.

III. In so far as the structural clue to the power elite today lies in the economic order, that clue is the fact that the economy is at once a permanent-war economy and a private-corporation economy. American capitalism is now in considerable part a military capitalism, and the most important relation of the big corporation to the state rests on the coincidence of interests between military and corporate needs, as defined by warlords and corporate rich. Within the elite as a whole, this coincidence of interest between the high military and the corporate chieftains strengthens both of them and further subordinates the role of the merely political men. Not politicians, but corporate executives, sit with the military and plan the organization of war effort.

The shape and meaning of the power elite today can be understood only when these three sets of structural trends are seen at their point of coincidence: the military capitalism of private corporations exists in a weakened and formal democratic system containing a military order already quite political in outlook and demeanor. Accordingly, at the top of this structure, the power elite has been shaped by the coincidence of interest between those who control the major means of production and those who control the newly enlarged means of violence; from the decline of the professional politician and the rise to explicit political command of the corporate chieftains and the professional warlords; from the absence of any genuine civil service of skill and integrity, independent of vested interests.

The power elite is composed of political, economic, and military men, but this instituted elite is frequently in some tension: it comes together only on certain coinciding points and only on certain occasions of 'crisis.' In the long peace of the nineteenth century, the military were not in the high councils of state, not of the political directorate, and neither were the economic men—they made raids upon the state but they did not join its directorate. During the 'thirties, the political man was ascendant. Now the military and the corporate men are in top positions.

Of the three types of circle that compose the power elite today, it is the military that has benefited the most in its enhanced power, although the corporate circles have also become more explicitly intrenched in the more public decision-making circles. It is the professional politician that has lost the most, so much that in examining the events and decisions, one is tempted to speak of a political vacuum in which the corporate rich and the high warlord, in their coinciding interests, rule.

It should not be said that the three 'take turns' in carrying the initiative, for the mechanics of the power elite are not often as deliberate as that would imply. At times, of course, it is—as when political men, thinking they can borrow the prestige of generals, find that they must pay for it, or, as when during big slumps, economic men feel the need of a politician at once safe and possessing vote appeal. Today all three are involved in virtually all widely ramifying decisions. Which of the three types seems to lead depends upon 'the tasks of the period' as they, the elite, define them. Just now, these tasks center upon 'defense' and international affairs. Accordingly, as we have seen, the military are ascendant in two senses: as personnel and as justifying ideology. That is why, just now, we can most easily specify the unity and the shape of the power elite in terms of the military ascendancy.

But we must always be historically specific and open to complexities. The simple Marxian view makes the big economic man the *real* holder of power; the simple liberal view makes the big political man the chief of the power system; and there are some who would view the warlords as virtual dictators. Each of these is an oversimplified view. It is to avoid them that we use the term 'power elite' rather than, for example, 'ruling class.'

*   *   *

The outermost fringes of the power elite—which change more than its core —consist of 'those who count' even though they may not be 'in' on given decisions of consequence nor in their career move between the hierarchies. Each member of the power elite need not be a man who personally decides every decision that is to be ascribed to the power elite. Each member, in the decisions that he does make, takes the others seriously into account. They not only make decisions in the several major areas of war and peace; they are the men who, in decisions in which they take no direct part, are taken into decisive account by those who are directly in charge.

On the fringes and below them, somewhat to the side of the lower echelons, the power elite fades off into the middle levels of power, into the rank and file of the Congress, the pressure groups that are not vested in the power elite itself, as well as a multiplicity of regional and state and local interests. If all the men on the middle levels are not among those who count, they sometimes must be taken into account, handled, cajoled, broken or raised to higher circles.

When the power elite find that in order to get things done they must reach below their own realms—as is the case when it is necessary to get bills passed through Congress—they themselves must exert some pressure. But among the power elite, the name for such high-level lobbying is 'liaison work.' There are 'liaison' military men with Congress, with certain wayward sections of industry, with practically every important element not directly concerned with the power elite. The two men on the White House staff who are *named* 'liaison' men are both experienced in military matters; one of them is a former investment banker and lawyer as well as a general.

Not the trade associations but the higher cliques of lawyers and investment bankers are the active political heads of the corporate rich and the members of the power elite. 'While it is generally assumed that the national associations carry tremendous weight in formulating public opinion and directing the course of national policy, there is some evidence to indicate that interaction between associations on a formal level is not a very tight-knit affair. The general tendency within associations seems to be to stimulate activities around the specific interests of the organization, and more effort is made to educate its members rather than to spend much time in trying to influence other associations on the issue at hand . . . As media for stating and re-stating the over-all value structure of the nation they (the trade associations) are important . . . But when issues are firmly drawn, individuals related to the larger corporate interests are called upon to exert pressure in the proper places at the strategic time. The national associations may act as media for co-ordinating such pressures, but a great volume of intercommunication between members at the apex of power of the larger corporate interests seems to be the decisive factor in final policy determination.'[2]

Conventional 'lobbying,' carried on by trade associations, still exists, although it usually concerns the middle levels of power—usually being targeted at Congress and, of course, its own rank and file members. The important function of the National Association of Manufacturers, for example, is less directly to influence policy than to reveal to small businessmen that their interests are the same as those of larger businesses. But there is also 'high-level lobbying.' All over the country the corporate leaders are drawn into the circle of the high military and political through personal friendship, trade and professional associations and their various subcommittees, prestige clubs, open political affiliation, and customer relationships. 'There is . . . an awareness among these power leaders,' one first-hand investigator of such executive cliques has asserted, 'of many of the current major policy issues before the nation such as keeping taxes down, turning all productive operations over to private enterprises, increasing foreign trade, keeping governmental welfare and other domestic activities to a minimum, and strengthening and maintaining the hold of the current party in power nationally.'[3]

There are, in fact, cliques of corporate executives who are more important as informal opinion leaders in the top echelons of corporate, military, and political power than as actual participants in military and political organizations. Inside military circles and inside political circles and 'on the sidelines' in the economic area, these circles and cliques of corporation executives are in on most all major decisions regardless of topic. And what is important about all this high-level lobbying is that it is done within the confines of that elite.

* * *

The idea of the power elite rests upon and enables us to make sense of (1) the decisive institutional trends that characterize the structure of our epoch, in particular, the military ascendancy in a

[2] Floyd Hunter, "Pilot Study of National Power and Policy Structures," Institute for Research in Social Sciences, University of North Carolina, Research Previews, II, March 1954, 8.

[3] *Ibid.*, 9.

privately incorporated economy, and more broadly, the several coincidences of objective interests between economic, military, and political institutions; (2) the social similarities and the psychological affinities of the men who occupy the command posts of these structures, in particular the increased interchangeability of the top positions in each of them and the increased traffic between these orders in the careers of men of power; (3) the ramifications, to the point of virtual totality, of the kind of decisions that are made at the top, and the rise to power of a set of men who, by training and bent, are professional organizers of considerable force and who are unrestrained by democratic party training.

Negatively, the formation of the power elite rests upon (1) the relegation of the professional party politician to the middle levels of power, (2) the semi-organized stalemate of the interests of sovereign localities into which the legislative function has fallen, (3) the virtually complete absence of a civil service that constitutes a politically neutral, but politically relevant, depository of brainpower and executive skill, and (4) the increased official secrecy behind which

great decisions are made without benefit of public or even Congressional debate.

As a result, the political directorate, the corporate rich, and the ascendant military have come together as the power elite, and the expanded and centralized hierarchies which they head have encroached upon the old balances and have now relegated them to the middle levels of power. Now the balancing society is a conception that pertains accurately to the middle levels, and on that level the balance has become more often an affair of intrenched provincial and nationally irresponsible forces and demands than a center of power and national decision.

But how about the bottom? As all these trends have become visible at the top and on the middle, what has been happening to the great American public? If the top is unprecedentedly powerful and increasingly unified and willful; if the middle zones are increasingly a semi-organized stalemate—in what shape is the bottom, in what condition is the public at large? The rise of the power elite . . . rests upon, and in some ways is part of, the transformation of the publics of America into a mass society.

Floyd Hunter

THE TOP LEADERS

In his study of regional cities, published in 1953, sociologist Floyd Hunter investigated decision-making on the local level. Employing role and status analysis and applying the model of a community power structure, he next turned his attention to the national scene with the publication of *Top Leadership, U.S.A.* In the following selection from that work, Hunter contends that a relatively small group of men formulate national policies within a power structure similar to that found in communities.

DURING the course of this study . . . I was seeking to learn whether there was a definable national power structure decisive in shaping the general

policy course of the country. With modifications that will be made later, I have found that there is such a power superstructure, generally with a coordination

From *Top Leadership, U.S.A.* by Floyd Hunter, 160, 163–168, 173–176, 179–180, 182–184, 186–189, 191 [Map on p. 185 and chart on p. 190 omitted]. Copyright © 1959 by The University of North Carolina Press. Reprinted by permission.

of goals and a resolution of unavoidable conflicts by the same types of individuals in roles and status positions similar to those found in communities. Utilizing the familiar sociological concepts of role and status analysis, together with questions related to group action patterns, I found it increasingly clear that the formulation of national policy and its ultimate execution by these individuals also were processes in a structure of action not unlike that found in community power situations.

*   *   *

Prestige from local status and power is a vital element in national power status. This does not mean that a man cannot become a national power figure without a local following, but without exception the men with whom I talked and who were designated by their peers as national power leaders were men quite stable in their positions as key figures in a localized configuration of activities. According to interests and capabilities, individuals are tapped from such positions for wider service in the cause of policy development. Few, indeed, are rootless men. Top leaders within basic, local power organizations are drawn into ever-widening circles of associations devoted to policy development.

It became apparent as national leaders were interviewed that all engaged in a kind of watchful observation of the movements of others. For example, all would know who recently had been elevated, demoted, or retired in any one of the larger corporations. If a man was about to retire in any of the larger enterprises, there would be a certain amount of speculation as to the man's successor. A man in the ascendance was called a "comer." Related business establishments would cultivate the goodwill of a comer, through channels.

In the local community, a man about to be elevated in an individual company is encouraged by his superiors to engage in one or more civic activities to enhance his community reputation. Such a man is aided in this endeavor by other members of the community, who become

fully aware of the fact that he is being groomed for bigger things. It becomes expedient for many to go along with the grooming process, sometimes even when they may entertain doubts about the fitness of a candidate.

This is also an important element of the informal national structure of power-wielding and policy-making. Entry into the circuit (not a tight circle) is by doing and sometimes by thinking. A man who is a doer is one in the upper ranks of leadership who actually may not do much of anything but talk with people and express his opinions on many different matters of public policy. He is often a person who earlier served varying periods of apprenticeship on national committees or in government service of the dollar a year variety, or who has come to be regarded as a lay expert on a specific topic such as education or international relations.

Inclusion in the upper power circuit is not a hard and fast, rigidly ruled process. Neither is exclusion. But there are some men known as recruiters of policy-making personnel. This is especially true in relation to government appointments. Two men, not a part of formal government, were mentioned very frequently as recruiters for key committees and government posts. But inclusion and exclusion, as processes in forming a trusted circuit within the national power structure, are not concerned only with the limits of government appointment.

*   *   *

In the process of evaluating a man's social status, there will have been much weeding out before a man reaches national prominence, and national groups are tolerant of numbers only to a point. The general top power structure is a cross-section affair, and any overload of representatives of minority groupings is avoided. With certain groups, inclusion is only token. Although ranking and exclusion are abhorrent to egalitarian concepts, they are functional to any power system.

The status claims of individuals have valid currency nationally if they bear the various seals of local approval. The right business, profession, style of life, manners, and morals are prerequisites to entry into the group of top level national policy makers. A leader may be a self-made man, a leader by achievement, or a leader by inheritance of status; he may be a leader by ascribed status, he may be a professional or a business enterpriser, and he may not be particularly rich; but to be on the inner councils of policy-making he must establish a claim of status as a leader in, or having vital connections with, an organization of men. He must also recognize the validity of the status claims at the national level of a broad range of other men active in key corporations, committees, government posts, and other institutional settings. If he does not recognize such claims, the general structure may discount his own claims and aid in tarnishing the brightness of his star within his own primary group. One man, a demoted executive of one of the national corporations, said as he looked over a list of leaders in the upper group of policy makers, "If I had played footsie with the guys on this list, I'd still be top man in my company. I should have got around to see them more, but I refused to believe they could shake me. I was twenty years younger then. I wouldn't make the same mistake now."

For this study to nail down the fact of recognition in status evaluations, three things were necessary to establish. First, men designated as top policy makers should know each other. I did not consider that knowing about others would be sufficient to contend that a power structure of top policy makers exists. Consequently, I asked those who were chosen by association groups as leaders to tell how many persons they knew on a list provided them. Secondly, they were to rate, by status, the persons they knew. And last, but most important, they must have acted with these others in developing specific policies. . . .

An analysis of the results of cross-country interviews, mailed questionnaires, and leadership polls conducted during the course of study showed that by 1956 out of several hundred persons named from all sources, between 100 and 200 men consistently were chosen as top leaders and were considered by all informants to be of national policy-making stature. One hundred of these received more votes proportionately than all others. These were also judged in the status-rating process as number-one power leaders. A second hundred were designated by the same informants as second raters. The remainder were either third raters or did not count at all in the opinion of the persons polled.

*   *   *

The structure of top number-one leaders tended toward closure. The number-one men knew number-one men. They recruited rising number-one leaders into their orbit and excluded those who did not fit. They knew generally the pattern of policy development, and they knew well and specifically how to go about getting what was good for them and for their individual enterprises. Their names appeared repeatedly in the national press. (Only twelve on a research list of 100 top leaders did not receive one or more press notices during the course of study up to 1956. It is likely that these twelve may have received notices that were missed.) They knew and were known by elected and appointed officials, from whom they tended to hold themselves somewhat superior and aloof. They represented a cross-section of national civic life. They belonged to clubs and associations in common membership across the nation. Their operating bases were located essentially in the large cities. They included the politicians, the men of wealth, and the military elite of whom Professor Mills speaks. None of these things can be said about the second and third raters, nor about all leaders examined in this study. In the cities, small towns, and states studied, connections between the upper leadership structures could be made, but the little fellows were excluded from the top leadership structure. The exclusion was made on a power status basis, not primarily on the basis of class position or institutional status. Inclusion in the top group of number-one leaders was, then, a rough measure of a man's power potential.

Let it be clearly understood again that I am not suggesting that the top leaders in the nation ever sit face to face around a table and decide in solemn judgment what will or will not be good for the nation. Such a view would deny the whole notion of process that is contained in the social power structure concept. Nor do I believe that much policy is ever wholly decided in smoke-filled rooms, nor in club leadership outings of the Aspen, Hot Springs, or Bohemian groups. No one-factor analysis is ever satisfactory, even though some articles that suggest this may appear from time to time in the sensational press. Yet, there is a selective process of agreement and habit patterns related to leadership recognition that can be observed. There is a kind of reservoir of leadership on tap from which men are chosen to perform the important tasks of policy-making and/or to give status to any major policy proposal. As one said, "Of course there is a group that's recognized as national leaders. They quietly put their stamp of approval on most of the things that go on. They're big men. You don't send a boy to do a man's job, you know."

I probed the notion that the men of family, wealth, and society prestige might be the true leaders of power in American society. I asked whether the managers had taken over. I questioned concerning the status of professional politicians in power-wielding. I wanted to know whether the country is run by powerful lobbies of labor and other special interest groups. I was interested in determining again whether the narrowed circle of men about whom I questioned represented a conspiracy of interests bent on doing the nation out of its birth-right.

The answers to all of these questions were qualified. "Yes, there is a definite number of men looked upon as being more powerful than others, but that answer is too simple. It does not explain power as a total thing." "Yes, some men of family and wealth are included, but there's more to a man's inclusion than

being born on the right side of town." "Yes, managers have taken over in many areas of influence, but they never act alone." "Yes, professional politicians and their political parties are important factors in policy-making and power, but they are a part of something bigger than pure politics." "Lobbies and their professional secretaries are very meaningful in decisions, but they are not always useful." "No, there is no conspiracy of interests. It is just natural that some men act the way they do, and most have the good of the country in mind."

Continuing to utilize the model of a community power structure in my interviews, I found certain common elements among the top leaders, whom I began to look upon as a national power structure, as they look upon themselves. I have already mentioned the facts that they knew each other, that they could rate each other in a status scale, and that they tended to include and exclude others from their company. They were not known to the little fellows on my lists of names nor did they know the little fellows, as pointed out. They represented a cross-section of national civic life, and active recruiting into the circuit goes on continuously to fill vacancies, geographic and otherwise. For the most part they tended to know certain persons in Congress and other national government policy posts. Their names appeared repeatedly in the national press as newsworthy spokesmen—particularly in crisis situations. There was a kind of amiable tolerance among them toward the world —a world that had been pretty good to them during the past few years. Importantly, they knew the patterns of the policy-making process and generally agreed on the content of such patterns. In the final analysis, of course, it is at the point of getting things done that a power structure is proved.

It will be remembered that I said hypothetically that at the national level of affairs, as in a local community, there is a power structure inside and outside government (but not synonymous with government or any other formal organization) acting in relation to policy development and that the national power structure could be identified in various ways. It is not a single pyramid of influence and authority. It is a kind of informal, potential group, representing many of the major influence groups, that acts on specific matters of policy as the need arises. And finally, although disagreements may occur in relation to specific issues, the basic values and aspirations of dominant interests, traceable most often to the larger corporate interests, will bring about a workable unity within the total power structure.

It was abundantly clear that the men interviewed did not think of government officials exclusively as top policy makers in the country. This does not say they did not recognize the important roles played by politicans in the process of getting things done, but universally, government was thought of as an instrument of extending policy rather than a primary source of policy development. It was taken for granted that government is extremely important. It was also taken for granted that organized government was but one of many power structures with which the men of national influence worked. Key men in government represent an apex of power, but in general it was assumed that these key men would act in concert and in accord with one or more other power groupings to formulate and extend policy.

*   *   *

The famous stag dinners of President Eisenhower were one important, informal gathering for hammering out a line for various policies. A large majority of the number-one leaders and second raters on my lists had attended these dinners. Such meetings with the President had not been confined to the Eisenhower administration. Mr. Truman had entertained many of the men on the number-one list. A high ranking Senator said that not too many people were aware of the fact that when Truman was President, informal, off-the-record gatherings were held at the White House. The guests went in the back door on regularly scheduled evenings. The Senator had met most of the top leaders outside and

inside government, at one time or another, at these meetings.

The development of policy requires such informal hashing. The process is the same as that which goes on in informal committee sessions daily in thousands of American communities. It is a part of a meeting of minds. Those who wished to be invited and were excluded were prone to say that something sinister was going on behind closed doors. It was insisted, however, that the White House discussions were open and not decisive. However, it was also apparent that some individuals in such meetings were listened to with considerably more interest than others. Labor was tolerated by some, for example, and second raters "sometimes talked too much."

The larger power interests had direct contact with government through the placement of dollar a year executives in key government spots. The same interests tended to find their way to key government committees, and there were close ties between these interests and the key cabinet posts.

A 1958 analysis of 99 number-one leaders in terms of their business and government connections showed that 17 of them had made a career of politics, 36 had never held either appointive or elective political office, but 46 had been in both business and government during their careers. The interchange between business and government was apparent, and the statistical findings were borne out by qualitative data.

"I have always considered myself above government and politics," said an executive of one of the largest service companies, who had just returned from a trip to Washington. "I do not go down to Washington very much. Not nearly so much as you might think," said another of the men in one of the biggest banks on Wall Street. "I was amused by one of the Texas newcomers the other day," he continued. "He came breezing into my office saying, 'I have just been down to see the President'—as if he had done something wonderful!"

"If I wanted to get something done through Washington, I would call up about six Senators that I know," said another man in a metal industry, "and I'd go down to Washington and see them. I'd also see a couple of cabinet members, as I did recently in relation to getting a fast write-off proposition through. I'd see two or three Congressmen, and come back home and wait for things to happen." He went on to say that he would not wait passively but would have some of his key men within his corporation follow through on the proposition. In other words, he would operate through several structures of power. He would not call for help from sources outside his immediate sphere of influence, he said, unless the situation got "sticky," i.e., unless he were thwarted—then he might begin the long process of building up pressure through committee activity, association work, political party pressure, and the like.

*   *   *

It must also be said that not all issues are decided by weight of numbers. Votes are not always counted in relation to issues. It is therefore important to policy makers to know whose word, timed right and spoken to the proper ear, will produce results. One man's making the right call to another may be more influential than countless ballots. This is especially true in those cases where elections are decided only on the basis of personalities and when such personalities will later decide the issues about which the voters did not trouble to inquire.

However, disagreement on a specific issue such as tariff did not mean that there was a lack of general accord on many basic matters of policy, and the mere fact that there was a show of strength on one side or the other helped to keep individuals within the general circuit of the top structure of policy-making.

Many men said that some of the top listed men represented the "committee person." The editor of a famous national daily newspaper, a paper that has a knack for choosing top names for its institutional articles, was one of those who recognized the validity of the executive committee status of many of the number-

one leaders. The committee persons are the type found on policy-making executive committees in communities and at the national level. They are opinion leaders, and they represent a reservoir of talent in policy-making. They may be asked to serve on important policy committees or to send representatives to them. They are tapped and they serve according to their interests in given subjects. They represent a cross-section of geographical groupings and formally organized groups.

The assumption that leaders coming into the power structure were recruited largely from the dominant urban centers was borne out. Of the number-one men, nine were from Chicago; six from New York; four from San Francisco; two each from Detroit, Los Angeles, Minneapolis, and Washington, D.C.; one each from Boston, Bridgeport (Conn.), Cincinnati, Dayton, Houston, and Pittsburgh. In the group of second raters, St. Louis led with six members; New York had five; Chicago, four; two members each came from Boston, Buffalo, and San Francisco; and one leader each was named from Birmingham, Denver, Fairmont (W. Va.), Glencoe (Ill.), Lexington (Ky.), Memphis, Minneapolis, Newark, New Orleans, Philadelphia, Poughkeepsie, and Washington, D.C.

The concentration of leadership in the major cities was noteworthy in the number-one group. In the second-rate group it tended to spread and reach down into the smaller cities. The third-rate group was even less concentrated and more diffuse. In this group, three leaders were from Chicago, and two each from Ann Arbor, Austin, New York, Oklahoma City, and Washington, D.C. The remainder of the third raters came from Birmingham (Ala.), Buffalo, Cambridge (Mass.), Casper (Wyo.), Dallas, Greensboro (N.C.), Indianapolis, Knoxville, Louisville, Maders (Calif.), Memphis, Morgantown (W.Va.), Newark, New Orleans, Rochester, Seattle, University (Miss.), Wake Forest (N.C.), and Washington, D.C.

The tendency toward decentralization of industrial complexes may have served to disperse national leadership, but with the example exceptions of the Dupont empire in Delaware and the Armstrong Cork Company of Pennsylvania, the large port cities and inland trading centers dominated the leadership picture. The dominant corporate groups within these cities furnished a large proportion of the top strata of policy makers. . . .

In one cross-country tour in which I stopped in a sample of twenty towns, large and small, by taking every tenth town designated on a road map, I found that the little fellows in the little towns knew directly scarcely any of the top persons listed, either personally or by hearsay. The returns of this investigation were so meager that presenting them in tabular form would be meaningless. The little fellows expect their political representatives or some local lawyer or corporate executive to do for them what they think they need done on matters of policy. They had little notion of the processes of power that go on in Washington, New York and abroad. Each little community had a miniature power structure within it—a stratification of local policy makers who by and large did hook up with top interests in their states. They recognized their own state industrial leaders, but the larger picture of the dynamics of policy development being outlined here was generally beyond their ken. Their outlet to the national power structure would appear to be through the restricted channels described in our model of state power and through association connections.

The sense of isolation from the centers of policy decision is one shared by many in American life—as a matter of fact, even by some of the very top leaders. Each thinks he is acting alone on many matters. Some feel that they are "voices crying in the wilderness."

There are sharp breaks in the communication networks. Even in well-organized industrial groupings like housing or textiles, communication through association meetings, letter writing, or trade bulletins always leaves some who claim never to have heard of a specific policy that might have been long in the making and finally put into operation. The bane of an association executive's existence is

the member who cries, "How did we ever get a policy like that? Who cooked that one up?" Groaning, the professional association leader is likely to ask himself, "Doesn't this fellow ever read? The policy he's talking about has been on page one of the bulletin for months!" Then aloud he will patiently explain to his member that the policy went through all the usual and proper steps of committee discussion and action.

Isolated or not, most community leaders have access to someone concerning specific issues that may trouble them. One way or another the policy matters that trouble John Q. Doakes get to the attention of one or another of the liaison leaders of the community in which he lives. Doakes is advised sometimes to go home and forget his troubles, but often his troubles are carried to some associated group as a case in point. The community policy needs become the seedbed of national policy decisions in a cumulative fashion. The chain of communication is crude, but socially significant policy impulses at the community level consistently light the circuits of the upper reaches of national policy-making.

It would appear upon observation that the community is the most focussed power unit in American society. Local coercion in the power framework is very obvious in case after case. However, as one moves out from individual community power structures into state, regional, industrial, or national power networks, the ability of small groups of men to act in strictly coercive relations to others outside the law seems more and more remote. The major coercive organs of power at the national level are two major configurations, formal government and the economic corporation. Both have organization structures that can reach down to the local level and exert coercive direction on individuals. In combination with other elements of organized community action the members of these two leading organs of power formulate national policy. . . .

Generally speaking, the Chamber of Commerce, various trade associations, and certain local leaders with some national prominence saw more clearly the dim avenues down which the majority of small town people viewed the larger national scene. Yet, what they read said that what happened at home was much more important than what was happening in New York or Washington. Some of the smaller local papers carried very little national news. How the news came to be news was a mystery beyond their comprehension and considered to be mainly outside their interests.

In looking over the list of top national leaders, one top local leader in Tennessee, a Chevrolet dealer, came to the name of Walter Reuther. He had passed over many other names with no comment. When he came to Reuther's name he said, seriously and earnestly perplexed, "It occurs to me I've heard that man's name somewhere, but I cannot rightly place him." When I told him of Reuther's auto union connections, he replied, "I guess I should have known that, selling automobiles. The name must have escaped me." The significance of the name Harlowe Curtice escaped him too. This case illustrates our hypothesis that "A large portion of the total power structure is not seen in operation because of its diffuse and informal characteristics," and the illustrations could be compounded.

*   *   *

The general pattern of action or the steps in process in the development of a given national policy, as given by the leaders, are these:

1. Establish the policy purpose and secure a dedication to this purpose by interested individuals.
2. Seek an unselfish working together of individuals and groups to achieve what they believe to be a policy direction for the good of the country.
3. Recruit successful men to help in furthering the idea.
4. Widen but restrict the circle of informed men.
5. Enlist the services of an established national organization in the cause, or set up a new organization if the existing organiza-

tions cannot embrace the new policy in their framework of action.
6. Utilize research to develop a factual base of operations.
7. Use a small but technically qualified group to give objective consideration and criticism to the facts.
8. Have facts and strategic problems analyzed by competent citizen groups.
9. Enlist public opinion through publicity of general news and special media.
10. Urge and re-urge vigorous support of all men who have knowledge of the program.
11. Use personal contact methods on other national leaders, the national administration, and Congress.
12. Appear publicly before committees of Congress or request hearings before administrative tribunals.
13. Be resolved to get action from the national administration.
14. Be resolved to get action from the houses of Congress.
15. Be prepared to use varying combinations of the above steps, and to begin over if not successful the first time.

From the other end of the matter, that is, from the men in the administration and Congress who are being pressured, at least three principles are guides, even though not always followed: (1) in advance of a decisive meeting, written recommendations should be circulated for study by the authoritative body, (2) all interested parties should be heard, and (3) the opportunity for rebuttal and appeal should be jealously guarded.

The nation's power system is a series of interlaced and co-ordinated power structures. Those at the apexes of power in communities, states, regions, service organizations, and industrial complexes become generally known to each other. Some of the leaders in the larger units of power become symbolic power figures in the nation. When such leaders think of policy directions and alternatives, they think of interrelated and weighted factors. Although individual units within the power system may appear to act in isolation, it is well known that major changes in pace and direction of any single power unit have profound effects on the whole.

Richard H. Rovere

THE AMERICAN ESTABLISHMENT

By the early 1960's, "the establishment" had entered the American vernacular. To some, it invoked visions of a mammoth, yet elusive body incorporating all individuals occupying positions of authority, of which the "power elite" comprised only a small segment of its overall structure. To others, these two terms seemed synonymous. In the selection below, Richard H. Rovere, free-lance writer and political commentator, discusses the goals and membership of the American establishment along with those groups in society tending to counteract its influence.

IT is now, of course, conceded by most fair-minded and objective authorities that there is an Establishment in America—a more or less closed and self-sustaining institution that holds a preponderance of power in our more or less open society. Naturally, Establishment leaders pooh-pooh the whole idea; they deny the Existence of the Establishment, and disclaim any connection of their own with it, and insist that they are merely citizens exercising citizens' rights and responsibilities. They often maintain that the real power is held by some other real or imagined force—the voters, the Congress, the comsymps, Madison Avenue, the rich, the poor, and so forth. This is an ancient strategy; men of power have always known how to use it. "Wouldst thou enjoy first rank?" St. John Chrysostom wrote. "Then cede it to another." *The News and Courier* is absolutely right.

Conceptions of the Establishment, to be sure, differ widely, just as do conceptions of the Church, the State, and other important institutions. Hilary Masters, a leading member of the Dutchess County school of sociologists, defined it in a recent lecture as "the legitimate Mafia." To William F. Buckley, Jr. and his collaborators on the *National Review* it is almost interchangeable with the "Liberal Machine," which turns out the "Liberal Line." Their Establishment includes just about everyone in the country except themselves, and the great hidden, enlightened majority of voters who would, if only they were given the chance, put a non-Establishment man in the White House and have John Kenneth Galbraith recalled from India, or left there and relieved of his passport. Galbraith, himself a pioneer in the field of Establishment studies, sees the Establishment as a rather small group of highly placed and influential men who embody the best of the Conventional Wisdom and can be trusted with substantial grants of power by any responsible group in the country. The perfect Establishment type, in his view, would be the Republican called to service in a Democratic administration (e.g., the present Secretary of the Treasury, Douglas Dillon) or the vice versa. "They are the *pivotal* people," he observed in one of his earlier studies. (The italics are his.) That was before his appointment as the Establishment's man in New Delhi. (He is not a member of his own Establishment, however, for he could not hope to be held over in a Republican administration.)

The fact that experts disagree on exactly what the Establishment is and how it works does not mean that they are talking about different things or about something that does not exist. Experts disagree about the Kingdom of God. This is not an argument against its existence; plainly the Kingdom of God is many things. Differences of opinion over the meaning of "justice" have given rise to one of the most honored professions in the world. One dogmatic Marxist may quarrel with another over the proper "role of the proletariat" and even about who should and who should not be counted as belonging to the "bourgeoisie." This does not make a fiction or a meaningless abstraction of either the proletariat or the bourgeoisie. The Establishment can be thought of in many different ways, all of them empirically valid in one or another frame of reference. Masters, Buckley, Galbraith, and Corradini look upon the Establishment from quite different points of view—which grow in the main out of their differing disciplines —but they would have no difficulty in agreeing that Douglas Dillon is true-blue or that, say, Senator Thomas J. Dodd of Connecticut is on the outside looking in —disapprovingly, in his case. Despite their differences of emphasis and approach, none of them would have many reservations about the *News and Courier*'s definition:

"The Establishment is a general term for those people in finance, business, and the professions, largely from the Northeast, who hold the principal measure of power and influence in this country irrespective of what administration occupies the White House. . . . [It is] a working alliance of the near-socialist professor and the internationalist Eastern banker calling for a bland bipartisan approach to national politics.[1]

For my own part, I think the definition is a pretty good one. I would cavil a bit at the notion that "the Establishment is a general term," etc. It is a good deal more than a collective noun, as I shall make clear. Moreover, there is a slight ambiguity in the phrase "principal measure of power." Too many journalists, awed by their observations of the Establishment at work, leap to the conclusion that its power is not only great but invariably decisive. This is by no means the case. There are powerful anti-Establishment forces at work, and frequently they pre-

vail. It seems to me perfectly clear, for example, that the Establishment has never found a way of controlling Congress. Indeed, there are times when Congress appears to be nothing more or less than a conspiracy to louse up the plans of the Establishment. Whatever the Establishment wants, it often seems, Congress mulishly opposes.

Nor has the Establishment ever made much headway in such fields as advertising, television or motion pictures. The basic orientation of the leaders in all these fields is anti-Establishment, and what Establishment strength exists is concentrated mainly on the lower levels —in advertising, the copywriters; in television, certain of the news departments (most notably at Columbia Broadcasting); and in the motion pictures, a few writers and actors. Still, Establishment strength in these areas is generally unimpressive. In Hollywood, to take a simple example, ICMPAFPWJ, the Independent Committee of the Motion Picture Arts for Freedom and Peace With Justice, an Establishment front, held a fundraising meeting in the Beverly Wilshire Hotel on November 20, 1961. Only twenty-eight persons attended, and the take for the evening, after eloquent pleas for support from Paul Newman and Joanne Woodward, was $3,067.50. (Of this amount, $2,900 was in the form of pledges, only about fifteen percent of which, in all likelihood, were actually redeemable.) On the very same evening, at the Beverly Hilton, the National Foundation for Amoebic Dysentery raised more than five times as much, all in cash or checks of that date, from three times as many people.

The Establishment does not control everything, but its influence is pervasive, and it succeeds far more often than its antagonists in fixing the major goals of American society. Though it does not, as I have noted, come anywhere close to controlling Congress, Congress is everlastingly *reacting* to it. Within the next couple of years, for example, Congress will spend a good part of its time fighting the Establishment program for a great revision of American trade practices and for eventual American associa-

[1] Charleston, South Carolina, *The News and Courier*, Oct. 18, 1961.

tion with the European Common Market. This whole scheme was cooked up at a three-day meeting of the Executive Committee at the Sheraton-Park in Washington immediately after President Kennedy's inauguration on January 20, 1961. The odds are heavily against the Establishment winning this battle in 1962 or even in 1963. The important thing, though, is that the Establishment has taken the initiative and put its great antagonist on the defensive. Practically everyone is agreed that in time the victory, even in this difficult matter, will go to the Establishment.

The Establishment is not, of course, at any level a membership organization in the sense that it collects dues, issues cards, or holds meetings openly under its own auspices. It is a coalition of forces, the leaders of which form the top directorate, or Executive Committee—referred to sometimes as "Central." At the lower levels, organization is quite loose, almost primitive in some cases, and this is one of the facts that explains the differences in definition among experts. In the upper reaches, though, certain divisions have achieved a high degree of organization. For instance, the directors of the Council on Foreign Relations make up a sort of Presidium for that part of the Establishment that guides our destiny as a nation. (The unimpeachable source, a dissident Executive Committee member who leaked the story about the Common Market decision, said that the Gist Subcommittee appointed to work on the Common Market matter had only two members not drawn from the Council.) The presidents and senior professors of the great Eastern universities frequently constitute themselves as *ad hoc* Establishment committees. Now and then, the Executive Committee regroups as an Establishment front for some particular end. In the summer of 1961, as a case in point, when anti-Establishment forces in Congress and elsewhere threatened the President's foreign-aid program, the Establishment, at the request of the White House, hastily formed the Citizens' Committee for International Development and managed to bull through a good deal of what the President wanted. The Estab-

lishment has always favored foreign aid. It is, in fact, a matter on which Establishment discipline may be invoked.

Summing up the situation at the present moment, it can, I think, be said that the Establishment maintains effective control over the Executive and Judicial branches of government; that it dominates most of American education and intellectual life; that it has very nearly unchallenged power in deciding what is and what is not respectable opinion in this country. Its authority is enormous in organized religion (Roman Catholics and fundamentalist Protestants to one side), in science, and, indeed, in all the learned professions except medicine. It is absolutely unrivaled in the great new world created by the philanthropic foundations—a fact which goes most of the way toward explaining why so little is known about the Establishment and its workings. Not one thin dime of Rockefeller, Carnegie, or Ford money has been spent to further Establishment studies.

If it were not for the occasional formation of public committees such as the Citizens' Committee for International Development, Establishment scholars would have a difficult time learning who the key figures are. Committee rosters serve Establishmentologists in the same way that May Day photographs of the reviewing stand above Lenin's tomb serve the Kremlinologists. By close analysis of them, by checking one list of names against another, it is possible to keep tabs quite accurately on the Executive Committee. A working principle generally agreed upon by Establishment scholars is this: If in the course of a year a man's name turns up fourteen times in paid advertisements in, or collective letters to, The New York *Times,* the official Establishment daily, it is about fourteen to one that he is a member of the Executive Committee. (I refer, naturally, to advertisements and letters pleading Establishment causes.) There are, to be sure, exceptions. Sometimes a popular athlete or movie actor will, innocently or otherwise, allow himself and his name to be exploited by the Establishment. He might turn up twenty times a year and still have no real status in the institution. But that is an exception. The rule is as stated above.

One important difference between the American Establishment and the party hierarchy in Russia is that the Establishment chairman is definitely *not* the man in the center of the picture or the one whose name is out of alphabetical order in the listings. The secret is astonishingly well kept. Some people, to be sure, have argued that when, as happens most of the time, the Establishment has a man of its own in the White House, he automatically becomes chairman just as he automatically becomes commander-in-chief of the Armed Forces. I am quite certain that this is not the case. For one thing, the Establishment rarely puts one of its tried and trusted leaders in the White House. Dwight Eisenhower and John F. Kennedy have both served the Establishment and been served by it, but neither is or ever was a member of the innermost circle. Both, indeed, were admitted with some reluctance on the part of senior members, and Eisenhower's standing has at times been most insecure.

I am not sure who the chairman of the Establishment is today, although I would not be altogether surprised to learn that he is Dean Rusk. By a thrust of sheer intuition, though, I did get the name of the 1958 chairman and was rather proud of myself for doing so. In that year, I discovered that J. K. Galbraith had for some time been surreptitiously at work in Establishment studies, and he told me that he had found out who was running the thing. He tested me by challenging me to guess the man's name. I thought hard for a while and was on the point of naming Arthur Hays Sulzberger, of The New York *Times,* when suddenly the right name sprang to my lips. "John J. McCloy," I exclaimed. "Chairman of the Board of the Chase Manhattan Bank, once with Cadwalader, Wickersham & Taft, and a partner in Cravath, de Gersdorff, Swaine & Wood, as well as, of course, Milbank, Tweed, Hope, Hadley & McCloy; former United States High Commissioner in Germany; former President of the World Bank; liberal Republican; chairman of the Ford Foundation and chairman—my God, how could I have hesitated!—of the Council on Foreign Relations, Inc.; Episcopalian." "That's the one," Galbraith said. He congratulated me for having guessed what it had taken him so much patient research to discover.

The Establishment is not monolithic in structure or inflexible in doctrine. There is an Establishment "line," but adherence is compulsory only on certain central issues, such as foreign aid. On economic affairs, for example, several views are tolerated. The accepted range is from about as far left as, say, Walter Reuther to about as far right as, say, Dwight Eisenhower. A man cannot be for *less* welfareism than Eisenhower, and to be farther left than Reuther is considered bad taste. Racial equality is another matter on which the Establishment forbids dissent. Opposition to integration is a cause for expulsion, or at least suspension for not less than a year, unless it is mere "token" opposition. The only *white* Southern members of the Establishment in anything like good standing are reconstructed Southerners or Southerners the Establishment has reason to believe would be reconstructed if political circumstances would allow it. Take Senator William Fulbright of Arkansas. He is a pillar of the Establishment even though he votes with the unenlightened on racial matters. The Council on Foreign Relations gave him an "A-1" rating when he was up for chairman of the Senate Foreign Relations Committee. The Executive Committee accepts him because it assumes his heart is in the right place. He is, after all, a former Rhodes scholar and a former university president. Moreover, the Fulbright scholarships have provided an enormous subsidy for Establishment intellectuals.

The Establishment has lately been having a most difficult time with those of its members—clergy, scientists, and academicians, in the main—who have joined the Committee for a Sane Nuclear Policy. The Executive Committee—in particular that powerful "hard-line" faction led by Dean Acheson and Roscoe Gist—has no use at all for this organization and would deal very sharply with its supporters if they did not include so many people who incorporate most of the Establishment virtues. Exactly what stand it will take remains to be seen.

In nonpolitical affairs, great doctrinal latitude is not only tolerated but encouraged. In religion, the Establishment is rigorously disestablishmentarian. Separatism is another matter on which discipline may be invoked. Like a citywide ticket in New York, the Executive Committee is carefully balanced religiously as well as racially. (The only important difference is that several places are kept for nonbelievers.) The only proscribed views are the noisier ones. Though he now and then gets an audience in the White House, Billy Graham is *persona non grata* in Establishment circles. Monsignor Fulton J. Sheen is regarded as a Catholic Billy Graham and is similarly a pariah.

Reinhold Niebuhr is the official Establishment theologian, and Bishop Angus Dun is the chaplain.

In matters of public policy, it may be said that those principles and policies that have the editorial support of The New York *Times* are at the core of Establishment doctrine. And those irregularities and eccentricities that receive sympathetic *consideration* in The *Times* (not only on the editorial page but in the Sunday Magazine and the Book Review) are within the range of Establishment doctrinal tolerance.

It is essential to an understanding of the Establishment to recognize its essentially *national* characteristics. *The whole of its power is greater than the sum of its parts.* Its leading figures have national and international reputations, but very often are persons of only slight influence or standing in the cities and states from which they come. Former Chairman McCloy, for example, cuts a lot of ice in Washington, Geneva, Paris, London, Rio de Janeiro, Bonn, Moscow, and Tokyo, but practically none in Manhattan. In Albany, he is almost unknown. The rela-

tive weakness of the Establishment in the states undoubtedly helps to explain the shellackings it repeatedly gets in Congress. Statewide—or one might say, statewise—it is often torn by a kind of factionalism that seldom afflicts its national and international operations. In New York, for example, Averell Harriman and Nelson Rockefeller have often found themselves locked in combat like Grant and Lee; in Washington, they are Alphonse and Gaston. And so it goes.

A state-by-state canvass of Establishment strengths and weaknesses was conducted by Perry Associates, a St. Louis firm, in 1959. Some of the highlights follow:

In three states—Texas, Oklahoma, and North Dakota—the Establishment is virtually outlawed. There are no restrictive or repressive measures on the statute books, but there is persistent harassment by police and other officials. The American Civil Liberties Union had expressed some interest in arranging a test case, but no suitable one was found. Despite constant police surveillance, there is considerable underground Establishment activity in the Dallas area and in San Antonio.

The Indiana authorities are openly hostile to the Establishment, and there has been continuing agitation for a law requiring Establishment agents to register with the Attorney General and be fingerprinted. It is hard to see what would be accomplished by this, for the Perry people could find no trace of Establishment activity anywhere in Indiana, except at Indiana University, in Bloomington. The faculty people there are state employees anyway and can quite easily be dealt with. In neither Nebraska nor Idaho could *any* Establishment influence be found. There were only the faintest traces in Wyoming, New Hampshire, Utah, and Florida.

Florida was the one Southern state in which Establishment forces seemed exceedingly weak. Elsewhere, it was learned, nearly all those who described themselves as "moderates" were actually connected with the Establishment.

The big centers are, as one might expect, the states with large cities and large electoral votes: New York, California, Illinois, Pennsylvania, Ohio, and Massachusetts. A rather surprising case, though, was Kansas, which ranked ahead of New Jersey and Maryland.

For some reason, Establishment studies have attracted few historians. Most of the work thus far has been undertaken by journalists, economists, sociologists, and psychologists. In consequence, very little has been done to uncover the origins of the Establishment. One British historian, Keith E. D. Smith-Kyle, maintains, in *America in the Round* (Polter & Polter, Ltd., London, 1956), that "the American pretense to equality was, to speak bluntly, given the lie by the formation in the early days of the Republic of the sort of 'command' group similar in most respects to what Britons nowadays speak of as 'The Establishment.' By 1847, when the Century Association was founded in New York, power had been consolidated in a handful of hands. From then on, whenever there was a 'laying on of hands,' the blood in those extremities was the very blood that had coursed through those that had molded the clay of life in the so-called Federal period."

It is plain that Smith-Kyle is trying to say, in a roundabout British way, that a hereditary aristocracy runs the show here. He is as wrong-headed in this matter as he is in most others. American students, though they number few trained historians among them and none of a celebrity that compares with Smith-Kyle's, subscribe almost unanimously to the proposition that the Establishment came into being at a far later date—to be exact, as well as neat, at the turn of the century. They see the institution forming during the administration of Theodore Roosevelt, who by common consent was the first Establishment President—and in a way the last. The Founding Fathers of today's group zeroed in on T. R. as if they had caught him in a perfect bombsight. Consider them all, a few of them still alive, all of them within living memory: Henry L. Stimson, William Allen White, Nicholas Murray Butler, Robert Frost, Albert Beveridge, Abraham Hum-

mel, Joseph Choate, William Travers Jerome, Jacob Riis, Charles Evans Hughes, Felix Frankfurter, Ida M. Tarbell, Joseph Pulitzer, Martin Provensen, Lincoln Steffens, Benson Frost, Learned Hand, W. Adolphe Roberts, Jane Addams, Nelson W. Aldrich, Eleanor Alice Burgess, John Hay, John Ray, John Jay Chapman, Van Wyck Brooks, Carl Schurz, Hamlin Garland, Oscar Straus, Winthrop Chanler, James R. Bourne, Whitelaw Reid, and Gifford Pinchot.

There, plainly, was the first Executive Committee!

Some uninformed publicists confuse the Establishment with the Organization. The two could not be more different. The Establishment Man and the Organization Man could not be more different, or more at odds. The Establishment uses the Organization from time to time, as a ruling group must in an industrial and commercial society. But it devoutly hopes that in time the Organization will wither away. The Organization would like to overthrow the Establishment. It had a near success when it ran its 1960 chairman, Richard M. Nixon, for President of the United States.

The New York *Times* has no close rival as an Establishment daily. Technological advance is making it possible for The *Times* to become a national newspaper. This development should add immeasurably to the growth of the institution's powers.

Most Establishment personnel get at least one newspaper besides The *Times*, in order to keep up with Walter Lippmann. Papers that carry both Lippmann and Joseph Alsop are in good standing with the Establishment and get a lot of advertising that way.

There are some specialized magazines but none of general circulation that can be described as official or semi-official organs. I have pondered long over the case of *Time* Magazine and have concluded that it has no real place in the Establishment. It goes too far in attacking Establishment positions and it has treated many Establishment members with extreme discourtesy and at times with vulgarity. The Establishment fears *Time*, of course, and it now and then shows cravenness in its attempts to appease it by putting Henry Luce on some commission or other (on freedom of the press, national goals, and so forth), or by giving his wife some political job. But the Luce publications generally must be considered as outside the Establishment.

Now that control of *Newsweek* has passed to Philip L. Graham, publisher of the Washington *Post,* it may be that the Establishment will adopt it as an official weekly.

U.S. News and World Report is widely read, but held in low regard.

Foreign Affairs has, within its field, the authority of *Pravda* and *Izvestia.*

Harper's, The Atlantic, and *The New Yorker* all have Establishment clienteles, but none can be regarded as official. The *Saturday Review* was once heavily patronized but no longer is. *The New Republic* is coming up. *The Nation* has long since gone down. A few of the younger Establishment intellectuals read *Partisan Review,* but the more sophisticated ones regard it as stuffy and prefer *The Noble Savage,* edited by Saul Bellow and issued in April and November by the World Publishing Company.

As Thomas R. Waring, the noted Southern journalist, has pointed out, "The significance of the Establishment can be discovered by finding out who is *not* a member." No one has yet compiled a complete list of nonmembers, but the following names may help significance seekers to get their bearings. These people are known to be nonmembers:

The Honorable Lyndon B. Johnson, Vice-President of the United States.

The Honorable Richard M. Nixon, former Vice-President of the United States.

The Honorable John Nance Garner, former Vice-President of the United States.

Cus D'Amato, prominent New York sportsman and manager of Floyd Patterson, the heavyweight champion of the world.

J. Edgar Hoover, Director, Federal Bureau of Investigation.

General of the Army Douglas MacArthur.

Allen Ginsberg, poet.

The Honorable James A. Farley, former Chairman, Democratic National Committee.

Fowler Harbison, President, Ramona College.

James Hoffa, President, International Brotherhood of Teamsters.

Hetherington Wells, Chairman of the Board, Consolidated Hydraulics, Inc.

Spruille Braden, diplomatist. (Here is a curious case indeed. Former Ambassador Braden has held many leading positions in the Establishment and is even now a member of the Council on Foreign Relations. But he is also a member of the national council of the John Birch Society. He was read out of the Establishment on April 14, 1960, before his John Birch connections were known.)

Sherman Adams, formerly the assistant to the President of the United States.

Drew Pearson, syndicated columnist.

Edgar Queeny, Chairman of the Board, Monsanto Chemical Corporation.

Charles Goren, bridge expert.

Charles A. Lindbergh, aviator.

The Honorable John MacCormack, Speaker, House of Representatives.

The Reverend Norman Vincent Peale, pastor, Marble Collegiate Church of New York (Dutch Reformed) and author of *The Power of Positive Thinking.*

Cyrus S. Eaton, industrialist and philanthropist.

The Honorable Everett McKinley Dirksen, United States Senator from Illinois and the minority leader of the Senate.

Dr. Edward Teller, nuclear physicist, often known as "Father of the Hydrogen Bomb."

Conrad Hilton, hotel executive.

The Honorable Richard J. Hughes, Governor of New Jersey.

Michael J. Quill, President, Transport Workers Union.

Morris Fishbein, M.D., editor and official, American Medical Association.

George Sokolsky, syndicated columnist.

Duke Snider, Los Angeles Dodgers.

John L. Lewis, President, United Mine Workers of America.

Carleton Putnam, writer, former Chairman of the Board, Delta Air Lines.

The Establishment has in its top councils some people who appear to the unsophisticated to be oppositionists. For example, Norman Thomas, the Socialist leader; Norman Mailer, the self-styled "hipster" novelist; and Norman Podhoretz, the firebrand editor of *Commentary* all enjoy close relations with leading figures on the Executive Committee. The Reverend Martin Luther King has been proposed for membership on the Executive Committee. On March 3, 1962, a planning committee that met for three days at the Royalton Hotel in New York reported that "we need informed, constructive criticism fully as much as we need support" and urged the recruitment of "people who will take a long, cold look at our policies and procedures and candidly advise us of any weaknesses they see. We recommend that in the cases of people playing this indispensable role of 'devil's advocate,' all discipline be suspended."

It is interesting to observe the workings of the Establishment in Presidential politics. As I have pointed out, it rarely fails to get one of its members, or at least one of its allies, into the White House. In fact, it generally is able to see to it that both nominees are men acceptable to it. It is never quite powerful enough, though, to control a nominating convention or actually to dictate nominations. National conventions represent regional interests much as Congress does, and there is always a good deal of unarticulated but nonetheless powerful anti-Establishment sentiment at the quadrennial gatherings of both Republicans and Democrats. Nevertheless, the great unwashed who man the delegations understand—almost intuitively, it seems—that they cannot win without the Establishment, and the more responsible among them have the foresight to realize that even if they did win they couldn't run the country without assistance from the Executive Committee. Over the years, a deal has been worked out that is almost an operating rule of American politics. The rule has been formulated by the

novelist Margaret Creal in this way:

When an Establishment man is nominated for the Presidency by either party, the Vice-Presidential candidate must be drawn from outside the Establishment. When, as has occasionally happened, the Establishment is denied the Presidential nomination, it must be given the Vice-Presidential nomination.

The system has worked almost perfectly for the last thirty years. In that time, the only non-Establishment man in the White House has been Harry Truman, and he had been Franklin Roosevelt's non-Establishment Vice-President. Putting Henry Wallace aside as a pretty far-out case and not counting Alben Barkley (a Vice-President's Vice-President), the Vice-Presidents have all been non-Establishment: John Nance Garner, Harry Truman, Richard Nixon, and Lyndon Johnson.

Now observe what happens when the Establishment has to yield first place, as it had to do at the Republican convention in 1960. Richard Nixon, a non-Establishment Vice-President, simply could not be denied the Presidential nomination. So the Establishment Republicans demanded and of course obtained Henry Cabot Lodge. There was a similar case in 1936, when the Republicans went outside the Establishment to nominate Alf Landon for first place. The Vice-Presidential candidate was Colonel Frank Knox, the publisher of the Chicago *Daily News*, and later Roosevelt's Secretary of the Navy. Four years later, the Establishment nominated Wendell Willkie on the Republican ticket and agreed to Charles McNary, distinctly non-Establishment. In 1944, it was Dewey (Establishment) and Bricker (Non). The Establishment was particularly powerful in 1948 and not only got Dewey again but Earl Warren. In 1952, the usual deal was made in both parties: Eisenhower versus Stevenson (Establishment) and Nixon and Sparkman (Non). Same thing in 1956, with Estes Kefauver in for Sparkman.

The Russians have caught on to the existence of the Establishment and understand some of its workings quite well. Nikita Khrushchev showed himself to be no slouch when he told Walter Lippmann, last spring, that President Kennedy was controlled by Nelson Rockefeller. Many people regarded this as depressing evidence of the grip of old-school Marxism on Khrushchev's mind. They thought he was mistaking a faded symbol of industrial and mercantile power for the real wielder of authority under People's Capitalism. He was doing nothing of the sort. He was facing the facts of Establishment life. Not as a Standard Oil heir but as an Establishment agent, Nelson Rockefeller had forced the Republicans to rewrite their platform so that it conformed very closely to Chester Bowles's Democratic platform and provided for a vigorous anti-Communist defense program. Where did the central ideas of both platforms originate? In—where else?—the studies made by the Rockefeller Panel for the Rockefeller Brothers Fund and published as *Prospect for America*. Who was on the Rockefeller Panel? Here are just a few of the names, left and right:

Dean Rusk
Chester Bowles
Jacob Potofsky
Anna Rosenberg
Henry Kissinger
(Director of the project)
                                 Lucius D. Clay
                                Arthur F. Burns
                                    Henry Luce
                             Oveta Culp Hobby
                                 David Sarnoff
And when Kennedy became President, from what foundation did he get his Secretary of State? The Rockefeller Foundation, of course.

David Riesman

THE VETO GROUPS

In this brief excerpt from *The Lonely Crowd*, sociologist David Riesman challenges both observers who attempt to apply the theories of Marx, Veblen, and others to contemporary society and those who search for a new elite. To Riesman, the realization that power has passed into the hands of numerous "veto groups" constitutes a major prerequisite for understanding the American political system.

IN terms of class, or elite theory, the first decades of American politics can be described as a period of conscious leadership by a mercantile-aristocratic group subject to occasional check, even displacement, by farmers and artisans who usually left politics alone. We might think of the latter as veto groups, and in that sense we can view the period between the end of the Civil War and 1900 as an exceptional period when the old veto groups were in retreat and the new ones had not yet found themselves. Yet, though the analogy between today and a hundred years ago is helpful, it conceals important differences in the mood and structure of the veto groups. Perhaps the most important change is the numerical elaboration and complexity of the latter and the fact that they not only exercise the residual veto of the farmer and artisan groups in the earlier period but also are constantly pressing their claims on the social and political sphere. These veto groups are lobbies, and also more than lobbies.

The shifting nature of the lobby, moreover, provides us with an important clue as to the difference between the present American political scene and that of the age of McKinley. Then there was conscious opposition to the ruling class on the part of those who at any moment wanted a better cut of the economic pie, and who were willing to follow another middle-class would-be elite to get it. In terms of cycles of participation and withdrawal from politics, the era was one in which the masses were drawn up into politics, but their entry was motivated by the search for opportunities to move up the class ladder. The people did not ask that politics be more fun, or provide more fun, but that it help them in their work and status.

To the participants, of course, it often looked as if there was a strong antibusiness movement. And in fact there were groups of moralizers who, through aristocracy or radicalism, were actually seeking a goal antithetical to that of the business class; the latter's leadership was so clear that these antibusiness groups could polarize their own destination by reference to the business position. But these fringe groups were actually quite weak, though they might find momentary resonance in groups of farmers or small businessmen.

With such exceptions, people arriving on the political scene felt themselves to be moving upward and onward. Where "up" and "on" lay, was clear. "Up" was up to the power and pelf of the business class. . . . "On" was on to the frontiers of production in a series of wars and skirmishes whose limits were set as clearly by the surrounding oceans as the limits of individual aspiration were set by the example of the business and political models of the day.

If we take a snapshot of the country in 1900, we see the South defeated and forgiven, the West bought off by remedial legislation, the world held at bay by the show of the Spanish War. Not before and not since has the class ladder seemed so straight, politics so crooked, and both so simply moralizable. . . .

The lobby in the old days actually ministered to the clear leadership, privilege, and imperative of the business ruling class. Today we have substituted for that leadership a series of groups, each of which has struggled for and finally attained a power to stop things conceivably inimical to its interests and, within far narrower limits, to start things. The movie-censoring groups, the farm groups and the labor and professional groups, the major ethnic groups and major regional groups, have in many instances succeeded in maneuvering themselves into a position in which they are able to neutralize those who might attack them. The very increase in the number of these groups, and in the kinds of interests "practical" and "fictional" they are protecting, marks therefore, a decisive change from the lobbies of an earlier day. There is a change in method, too, in the way the groups are organized, the way they handle each other, and the way they handle the public, that is, the unorganized.

These veto groups are neither leader-groups nor led-groups. The only leaders of national scope left in the United States today are those who can placate the veto groups. The only followers left in the United States today are those unorganized and sometimes disorganized unfortunates who have not yet invented their group.

Within the veto groups, there is, of course, the same struggle of antagonistic cooperators for top places that goes on in other bureaucratic setups. *Among* the veto groups competition is monopolistic; rules of fairness and fellowship dictate how far one can go. Despite the rules there are, of course, occasional "price wars," like the jurisdictional disputes of labor unions or Jewish defense groups; these are ended by negotiation, the division of territory, and the formation of a roof organization for the previously split constituency. These big monopolies, taken as a single group, are in devastating competition with the not yet grouped, much as the fair-trade economy competes against the free-trade economy. These latter scattered followers find what protection they can in the interstices around the group-minded.

Each of the veto groups in this pattern is capable of an aggressive move, but the move is sharply limited in its range by the way in which the various groups have already cut up the sphere of politics and arrayed certain massive expectations behind each cut. . . .

By their very nature the veto groups exist as defense groups, not as leadership groups. If it is true that they do "have the power," they have it by virtue of a necessary mutual tolerance in which each of these groups allows all the other groups to dominate its agenda of attention. More and more they mirror each other in their style of political action, including their interest in public relations and their emphasis on internal harmony of feelings. There is a tendency for organizations as differently oriented as, say, the Young Socialists and the 4-H Club, to adopt similar psychological methods of salesmanship to obtain and solidify their recruits.

. . . Character structure by no means determines vote, opinion, or informedness but is, on the contrary, an influence that tends to cut across party and opinion lines. So it is likewise clear that the veto groups are not formed along the lines of character structure either. . . . The smaller the constituency, of course, the smaller the number of veto groups involved and the greater the chance that some one of them will be dominant. Thus, in local politics there is more indignation and less tolerance, just as even the *Chicago Tribune* is a tolerant paper in comparison with the community throwaways in many Chicago neighborhoods.

The same problem may be considered from another perspective. Various groups have discovered that they can go quite far in the amorphous power situation in America without being stopped. Our society is behaviorally open enough to permit a considerable community of gangsters a comfortable living under a variety of partisan political regimes. In their lack of concern for public relations these men are belated businessmen. So are some labor leaders who have discovered their power to hold up the economy, though in most situations what is surprising is the moderation of labor demands—a moderation based on psycho-

logical restraints rather than any power that could effectively be interposed. Likewise, it is sometimes possible for an aggressive group, while not belonging to the entrenched veto-power teams, to push a bill through a legislature. Thus, the original Social Security Act went through Congress, so far as I can discover, because it was pushed by a devoted but tiny cohort; the large veto groups including organized labor were neither very much for it nor very much against it.

For similar reasons those veto groups are in many political situations strongest whose own memberships are composed of veto groups, especially veto groups of one. The best example of this is the individual farmer who, after one of the farm lobbies has made a deal for him, can still hold out for more. The farm lobby's concern for the reaction of other veto groups, such as labor unions, cuts little ice with the individual farmer. This fact may strengthen the lobby in a negotiation: it can use its internal public relations problems as a counter in bargaining, very much as does a diplomat who tells a foreign minister that he must consider how Senator McKellar will react. . . .

Nevertheless, people go on acting as if there still were a decisive ruling class in contemporary America. Recent investigations show that businessmen think labor leaders and politicians run the country. Labor and the left think that "Wall Street" runs it, or the "sixty families." Wall Street, confused perhaps by its dethronement as a telling barometer of capital-formation weather, may think that the midwestern industrial barons, cushioned on plant expansion money in the form of heavy depreciation reserves and undivided profits, run the country. They might have some evidence for this in the fact that the New Deal was much tougher with finance capital—e.g., the SEC and the Holding Company Act— than with industrial capital and that when, in the undistributed profits tax, it tried to subject the latter to a stockholder and money-market control, the tax was quickly repealed. . . .

If businessmen *feel* weak and dependent they *are* weak and dependent, no matter what material resources may be ascribed to them. My impression, based mainly on experiences of my own in business and law practice, is that businessmen from large manufacturing companies, though they often talk big, are easily frightened by the threat of others' hostility; they may pound the table, but they look to others for leadership and do not care to get out of line with their peer-groupers. Possibly, attitudes toward such an irascible businessman as Sewell Avery might mark a good dividing line between the older and the newer attitudes. Those businessmen who admire Avery, though they might not dare to imitate him, are becoming increasingly an elderly minority, while the younger men generally are shocked by Avery's "highhandedness," his rebuff of the glad hand.

Furthermore, reading accounts in court records of negotiations between little businessmen and gangsters, I have been struck by the resemblance in the mood of their negotiations to the negotiations, say, of big businessmen and labor leaders. These small businessmen sat around in night clubs and taverns and exchanged small talk with the milk, trucking, or other racketeers to whom they were paying tribute. An air of pleasant sociability hung, like tobacco smoke, over the proceedings. Of course these gangsters not only had the power but showed it by occasionally bombing an uncooperative factory or overturning an uncooperative truck. But the gangsters, being illegal, had to use such methods to establish themselves as a veto group. In the big leagues of the big veto groups the limits of power are seldom tested by combat though this restraint, resting, as I think, on psychological grounds, is easily rationalized in terms of power politics and public relations.

Businessmen, moreover, are not the only people who fail to exploit the power position they are supposed, in the eyes of many observers, to have. Army officers are also astonishingly timid about exercising their leadership. During the war one would have thought that the army would be relatively impervious to criticism. But frequently the generals went to great lengths to refrain from doing something about which a congressman might make an unfriendly speech. They did so even at times when they might have brushed the congressman off like an angry fly. When dealing with businessmen or labor leaders, army officers were, as it seemed to me, astonishingly deferential; and this was as true of the West Pointers as of the reservists. Of course, there were exceptions, but in many of the situations where the armed services made concessions to propitiate some veto group, they rationalized the concessions in terms of morale or of postwar public relations needs or, frequently, simply were not aware of their power position.

To be sure, some came to the same result by the route of a democratic tradition of civilian dominance. Very likely, it was a good thing for the country that the services were so self-restrained. I do not here deal with the matter on the merits but use it as an illustration of changing character and changing social structure. . . .

As things are today, however, most observers seem unwilling to take a straight look at the amorphous distribution of power in America. Sophisticated social scientists pin their hopes or fears on this or that elite, echoing the bottom dogs who feel there is a boss somewhere. Yet people fail to see that, while it may take leadership to start things running, or to stop them, very little leadership is needed once things are under way—that, indeed, things can get terribly snarled up and still go on running. If one studies a factory, an army group, or other large organization, one wonders how things get done at all, in view of the lack of leadership and the extensive featherbedding. . . . At any rate, the fact they do get done is no proof that there is someone in charge. Power in America seems to me situational and mercurial; it resists attempts to locate it the way a molecule, under the Heisenberg principle, resists attempts simultaneously to locate it and time its velocity.

There are, of course, still some veto groups that have more power than others and some individuals who have more power than others. But the determination of who these are has to be made all over again for our time: we cannot be satisfied with the answers given by Marx, Mosca, Michels, Pareto, Weber, Veblen, or Burnham, though we can learn from all of them. Paradoxically, it may be that while the mesas of the veto groups have replaced the mountain peaks of class in the United States, power has nevertheless become more concentrated in another respect, namely in the decline of the older separations of power, both constitutional and social-psychological. Most of the constitutional separations—executive, legislative, and judicial; upper chamber and lower chamber; federal and state—are of diminishing importance. So are the social-psychological separations that formerly buttressed the political ones: the separations between those who sought power through wealth and wealth through power; between those locally oriented and those nationally oriented; between those who looked to business models and those who looked to agrarian ones.

*   *   *

Rather, power on the national scene must be viewed in terms of issues. It is possible that, where an issue involves only two or three veto groups, themselves tiny minorities, the official or unofficial broker among the groups can be quite powerful—but only on that issue. However, where the issue involves the country as a whole, no individual or group leadership is likely to be very effective, because the entrenched veto groups cannot be budged: unlike a party that may be defeated at the polls, or a class that may be replaced by another class, the veto groups are always "in." . . .

Does not wealth, one might ask, exert its pull in the long run? In the past this has been so; for the future I doubt it. The future seems to be in the hands of the small business and professional men who control Congress: the local realtors, lawyers, car salesmen, undertakers, and so on; of the military men who control defense and, in part, foreign policy; of the big business managers and their lawyers, finance-committee men, and other counselors who decide on plant investment and influence the rate of technological change; of the labor leaders who control worker productivity and worker votes; of the black belt whites who have the greatest stake in southern politics; of the Poles, Italians, Jews, and Irishmen who have stakes in foreign policy, city jobs, and ethnic religious and cultural organizations; of the editorializers and storytellers who help socialize the young, tease and train the adult, and amuse and annoy the aged; of the farmers—themselves a warring congeries of cattlemen, corn men, dairymen, cotton men, and so on—who control key departments and committees and who, as the living representatives of our . . . past, control many of our memories; of the Russians and, to a lesser degree, other foreign powers who control much of our agenda of attention; and so on. The reader can complete the list.

But people are afraid of this indeterminacy and amorphousness in the power situation. Even those intellectuals, for instance, who feel themselves very much out of power and who are frightened of those who they think have the power, prefer to be scared by the power structures they conjure up than to face the possibility that the power structure they believe exists has largely evaporated. This is of course partly because if someone has power, one can always imagine taking it away from him.

Arnold M. Rose

THE POWER STRUCTURE

The late Arnold M. Rose first received public recognition as a sociologist in 1944, when he and Richard Sterner assisted Gunnar Myrdal in the publication of *An American Dilemma*. In this selection from *The Power Structure*, he rejects the theory of a monolithic elite as a simplistic explanation of the decision-making process. Rose visualizes a multiplicity of elites representing all aspects of organized human activity, each group essentially confining operations to a small sector of society.

THE belief that an "economic elite" controls governmental and community affairs, by means kept hidden from the public, is one that can be traced at least as far back in American history as the political attacks of some Jeffersonians on some Hamiltonians at the end of the eighteenth century. Scarcely any lower-class political movement in the United States has failed to express the theme that the upper classes successfully used nondemocratic means to thwart democratic processes. Perhaps the widest popular use of the theme was achieved by the Populist movement in the decades following 1890. Anarchism and Marxism were imports from Europe that accepted the theme as one of the essential elements of their ideologies. The history of the United States also provides ample factual examples to strengthen credence in the theme. The literature of exposure, especially that of the "muckrakers" in the first decade of the twentieth century, provides details as to how economically privileged individuals and groups illegally bought and bribed legislators, judges, and executive heads of government to serve their own desires for increased wealth and power.

The belief is not entirely wrong. But it presents only a portion of relevant reality and creates a significant misimpression that in itself has political repercussions. A more balanced analysis of the historical facts would probably arrive at something like the following conclusion: Seg-

ments of the economic elite have violated democratic political and legal processes, with differing degrees of effort and success in the various periods of American history, but in no recent period could they correctly be said to have controlled the elected and appointed political authorities in large measure. The relationship between the economic elite and the political authorities has been a constantly varying one of strong influence, co-operation, division of labor, and conflict, with each influencing the other in changing proportion to some extent and each operating independently of the other to a large extent. Today there is significant political control and limitation of certain activities over the economic elite, and there are also some significant processes by which the economic elite uses its wealth to help elect some political candidates and to influence other political authorities in ways which are not available to the average citizen. Further, neither the economic elite nor the political authorities are monolithic units which act with internal consensus and co-ordinated action with regard to each other (or probably in any other way). In fact there are several economic elites which only very rarely act as units within themselves and among themselves, and there are at least two political parties which have significantly differing programs with regard to their actions toward any economic elite, and each of them has only a partial degree of internal cohesion. On domestic issues, at least, it is appropriate to observe that there are actually four political parties, two liberal ones and two conservative ones, the largest currently being the national Democratic party, which generally has a domestic policy that frustrates the special interests of the economic elite. This paragraph states our general hypothesis, and we shall seek to substantiate it with facts that leave no significant areas of omission. Merely to provide it with a shorthand label, we shall call it the "multi-influence hypothesis," as distinguished from the "economic-elite-dominance" hypothesis.

*   *   *

Most aspects of power have remained sufficiently stable for a student of the power structure to draw generalizations and to note slow-moving trends. In contrast to the major theses of C. Wright Mills and Floyd Hunter—that there is a secret, hierarchical, and unified power structure in the United States headed by an economic elite, that the political elite occupies only a secondary position in the power structure, and that the masses are apathetic and act in terms of false consciousness of their interests—we would assert the following propositions. . . .

1. There is a power structure in every organized activity of American life and at every level—national, regional, state, and local. Power is the major means used by a large, heterogeneous society to effect or to resist change, and—except in simple face-to-face relations—power is structured, which is to say that there are different roles and role relationships, and a pattern into which these roles and relationships fit.

2. There are varying degrees of relationship and agreement among these varied power structures. They are certainly not unified into a simple power structure, even *within* the categories of the economic and the political, although occasionally semi-permanent liaisons develop among them. Nor are they usually countervailing, because each operates primarily within its own sphere of influence, although countervailing (or check-and-balance) relationships occasionally do occur. The political party power structures—there are at least four major ones on the national level alone—probably have the largest number of relationships with other power structures, both because one of their specific roles is to mediate conflicts and because they have a large degree of control over the bureaucratic machinery of government, which —in turn—monopolizes most of the instruments of organized physical force.

3. Within each power structure, a small number of persons hold the largest amount of power. In community studies, this has been estimated to constitute less than 1 per cent of the population, but such estimates refer to those who lead in community-wide political decisions, and not to power *within* the spheres of business, unions, voluntary associations, schools, churches, etc. While in any sphere of activity there are "leaders," who constitute a tiny proportion of all those affected by the activity, this does not mean that the others have no power whatsoever. Opposition groups occasionally form, and sometimes succeed in overturning the existing elite. In all cases where there are elections, the rank-and-file voters exercise some restraining and modifying power over the elite. Their power is a function of the extent to which they have interacted to create a public opinion, the extent to which the election machinery is honest, and the extent to which voters are equal. Under these criteria, most governmental elections accord a good deal of power to the electorate, most business corporation elections accord practically no power to the electorate, and labor union and voluntary association elections vary between these two poles. But even in government and in actively democratic trade unions, there is an ever-changing elite which exercises most of the power at any given moment.

4. Each elite manifests its power mainly within its own domain. That is, the strongest powers of businessmen are exercised within their own businesses, and the strongest powers of politicians and public administrators are exercised within government. But particularly the political and economic elites, among all

the elites, influence each other's spheres. Especially since the 1930's the government has set various restrictions and controls on business, and has heavily taxed business and the public to carry out purposes deemed to be for the general good—welfare programs, education programs, highways, war and military defense activities, etc. Business leaders use lobbyists, "business representatives" in legislatures, contributions to campaign funds, publicity designed to influence public opinion, the "political strike," and other lesser techniques to influence government. Businessmen influence government more effectively than most non-businessmen—not only because they can afford lobbyists, advertisements and other costly techniques—but also because they are more educated, more knowledgeable, more articulate, and more activist than average citizens. The latter qualities give them an advantage quite compatible with a democratic society.

5. The economic elite has its greatest success in influencing government where there are no counter-pressures—from other sectors of the economic elite, from other non-economic elites, and from public opinion. The result has been that the economic elite has been relatively successful in influencing government purchasing agents and the independent regulatory commissions. This is not quite an accurate way of stating the facts, however, since individual businesses often compete strongly with each other in influencing these factors of government, and there is a considerable turnover in the individual businesses benefited by these sectors of government. In pressuring or appealing to the top levels of the federal administration, to the Congress, or even to many state legislatures (especially outside the South), businessmen have been much less successful since the 1930's. In fact, as far as general legislation is concerned, they have had an almost unbroken series of defeats, although they have succeeded in *delaying* the passage of certain bills for years. Thus, while businessmen have gained certain economic benefits from government, their typical ideology—in

favor of businessman leadership in the society and of a minimum of government activity for the benefit of other segments of the population—has made no progress.

6. While the federal government has been gaining ascendancy over the state and local governments, and while the office of the President has been gaining power at the expense of Congress, it is far from true that the state governments and the Congress are powerless. Rather, it could be said that the "balance of power" doctrine envisaged in the Constitution has come into operation only since 1933, because the federal government (except for military activities) and the presidency (except in wartime) were relatively weak institutions before then. These two trends in political power have reduced the influence of the economic elite, for the federal government is less susceptible to influence from businessmen than are most of the state governments, and the presidency is less susceptible to such influence than are many of the congressmen.

7. In the early 1960's a coalition of several decades' duration between two major political power structures—the conservative leadership of the Republican party and the Democrats in power in most of the Southern states—largely broke down. The Southern Democrats, changing in membership and reduced in number by Republican inroads on their constituencies, drew closer to the Northern Democrats, except publicly over the issue of civil rights. The South was rapidly becoming like the North—in its industrialization, urbanization, patterns of race relations permitted by Negro voting, and development of a two-party system. The Republican party was sharply divided between its conservatives and liberals, on the one hand, and a smaller group of right-wing extremists with a vigorous ideology who seized control of the party's grassroots structures in the majority of states. The extremists—while occasionally ideologically supportive of business—were not as willing to make political compromises in behalf of business or as willing to trust leading businessmen, as had been the previous con-

servative leaders of the Republican party. All these developments, coupled with the political skill of President Lyndon B. Johnson, permitted the passage of a great deal of "liberal" legislation in the 1964–65 sessions of Congress—including "Medicare" for the elderly . . . , federal aid to education, the anti-poverty program, tax reduction without a balanced budget, a comprehensive civil rights act, a voting rights act, elimination of national quotas for immigrants, creation of a new Department of Housing and Urban Development, aid to urban mass-transit programs and to highway and city beautification efforts, and a National Foundation on the Arts and Humanities. Further, the President had an unofficial price control policy which worked for a few years to keep major industries from raising prices.

8. In the passage of the above-mentioned legislation, interested economic elite pressure groups were mostly defeated. On the other hand, the major legislation sought by organized labor—repeal of Section 14(b) of the Taft-Hartley Act—was also defeated in the Senate. The one economic elite group that continued to reap major economic benefits from government activity was the armaments and space-exploration supply industries, although the Secretary of Defense made certain decisions on procurement—such as in favor of competitive bidding rather than cost-plus contracts—even in this area which were not favored by the leading manufacturers.

9. Through the Voting Rights Act of the Congress and the *Baker* v. *Carr* and *Reynolds* v. *Sims* decisions of the United States Supreme Court—including the giving of permission to the Attorney General to seek a Court review of the poll tax (which was consequently outlawed by the Supreme Court)—a major democratization of voting for state legislatures was occurring in many states. Both state and local government activities were increasingly influenced by standards set by federal aid programs that covered ever wider spheres.

10. The pattern of legislation at both federal and state levels revealed the emergence of new popular pressure groups with considerable power, partly because of demographic shifts and partly because of growing political consciousness among these groups. These groups are the elderly, a portion of whom are now organized into many associations, the most politically active of which is the National Association of Senior Citizens; the Negroes, possibly a majority of whom are organized into various civil rights associations and activist churches; and the "resentful disaffecteds," practically all organized into a variety of leftist and rightist extremist organizations, of which the John Birch Society is the largest and the wealthiest. . . .

11. The major area of small-group control of national policy remaining in the country was that of foreign policy. The most powerful arm of this small group—namely the President and his official advisers—are quite exposed to the public. But there are secret decision-makers operating in this area also—secret in that their influence and processes of decision-making are not accessible to the public. These decision-makers are the CIA, the foreign policy "experts" in the universities and in such organizations as the Foreign Policy Association and the Council on Foreign Relations, and the military supplies industrialists who exert their influence mainly through the military leaders. The last-named are the ones whom Mills placed at the pinnacle of the power elite in the United States; we identify them rather as one influence among several affecting the nation almost exclusively in the area of foreign policy. We are entirely skeptical about Mills's contention that the other "members" of the economic elite—say, for example, those organized in the Chamber of Commerce—have more influence on foreign policy than the workers organized into trade unions, especially when they engage in shipping boycotts.

12. Despite the fact that the Republican party's ideological move to the right after 1962 left the Democrats securely in command of the center, the program of the Democratic party remained as liberal as it had ever been. This can be seen not only by comparing national party plat-

forms over the years, but by reviewing the legislation supported (and usually passed) by the majority of Democrats in Congress and by the Democratic Presidents Kennedy and Johnson. This can be explained either as a long-run trend—in terms of the increasing strength of voters who favor liberal measures and generally support the Democratic party as the instrument to achieve them—or as part of a structural cycle. Lipset specifies a version of the latter theory: Republican Presidents seek center support and so force Republican congressmen from safe conservative seats to behave in a more liberal fashion. When a Republican holds the presidency, the Southern contingent of conservative Democrats have more power in their party. Thus, in a Republican presidency, the two congressional parties are not so far apart. But when a Democrat holds the presidency, he pulls his congressmen to the left, to respond to the needs of the greater number of voters there, while the Republican congressmen are free to follow their ideological inclination toward the right, and the two parties are quite far apart. It is difficult to judge from the facts which theory is correct, but this author tends to regard the former theory as more persuasive, especially in view of the decline of differences between South and North. In any case, there has been a significant difference between the platforms and policies of the two national parties at least since 1932, and the difference in the mid-1960's was as great as could be found between democratic political parties anywhere in the Western world. The increasing number of differences between the two major political parties, and the growing ideological framework for those differences, will probably have profound implications for the political future of the United States—but it is still too early to foresee the future development. Nevertheless, from the standpoint of the thesis of this book, we can say that there is little evidence that business is playing any significant role in the development of these trends. Business is a declining influence on the political power structures, except in the narrow area of its relationship to government procurement

officials and the independent regulatory commissions—largely because business exerts its strongest efforts on these and because there are few countervailing influences on them. . . .

13. The public's and the formal leadership's image of the power structure—if we can generalize from a study of the one state of Minnesota—does not include many people as seeing the economic elite as all-powerful, although the extent to which they do see business as influential may be somewhat exaggerated in terms of the facts. Judging from their public pronouncements, it is the political extremist—of both the right and the left—whose image of the American power structure includes a conspiratorial and all-powerful role for the economic elite. The extremist groups have different names for this "all-powerful group" but they refer to the same business elite: The "lunatic fringe" rightists call them "the hidden group behind the communists," the more rational extreme rightists call them "the Establishment"; the more rational extreme leftists also call them "the Establishment" or "Wall Street," but are more likely to use the Mills-Hunter terms "the power elite" or "the power structure," while the less rational extreme leftists either use the same terms or refer bluntly to "the big business conspiracy." While it is of considerable interest that the political extremists of both right and left—apparently along with many non-extremist intellectuals influenced by Mills and Hunter—have the same image of the top business elite as being all-powerful, it is of greater importance to note that the majority of the people and of the positional leaders of American organized society do not have this image. We have adduced much evidence in this book that the top business elite are far from having an all-powerful position; that power is so complicated in the United States that the top businessmen scarcely understand it, much less control it; and that since 1933 the power position of businessmen has been declining rather than growing.

14. Because the spheres of their organizations have grown in recent decades, the elites of the federal adminis-

tration (including the military), of the federal courts, of certain voluntary associations, and of certain education and scientific institutions, have grown more powerful. While on rare occasions they supersede in power the top political elites —as when the United States Supreme Court ordered the state governments to end racial segregation and to reapportion their legislatures in accord with population, or when the same Court declares unconstitutional a federal statute, or when the civil rights associations pressure Congress into voting for a statute as sweeping as the Civil Rights Act of 1964, or when the labor and old-age groups pressure Congress into voting for a statute as sweeping as the Medicare Act of 1965 (although both these statutes had the full support of that significant political elite—the President)—the political elites are usually ascendent over them. The political elites control the agencies of force and the instruments of legislation, have considerable access to the mass media, and have the support of public opinion. The political elites—the two major parties, the President, the factions in the houses of Congress, the executives and legislatures of the states and large cities—are not unified of course, and they check-and-balance each other to a considerable extent.

15. While the two major political parties are listed by us as among the most powerful groups in the United States, their structures are quite generally misunderstood by the public and by non-specialized intellectuals and other leadership groups. They are structured mainly as voluntary associations, with grassroots elections that range from being wholly democratic to being "controlled" from a self-perpetuating group at the top. In some states (e.g. Texas) they are highly fractionated and schismatic. They are structured on the layer principle: ward or county, municipality, district, and state. They scarcely exist as voluntary associations at the national level— except for the quadrennial national nominating conventions—but they exist in the caucuses of Congress, where they are the most important single influence on congressmen's voting behavior despite the bifurcation within both political parties.

16. While money in the hands of rich people opens special opportunities to democratic political processes—such as through the use of lobbyists, advertisements, and campaign contributions— these processes are by no means closed to poor people. A volunteer campaign worker for a congressman will have more influence on him than most lobbyists, and as much influence on him as a campaign contribution equivalent to the voluntary labor, roughly speaking. The fact that the political party in most states is an open, if not entirely democratic, voluntary association, and the fact that it is the single most important influence on most elected officials, also gives the non-wealthy citizen access to political power often greater than that of the wealthy, but not politically active, citizen. In this context it should be understood that most elected officials, especially at higher levels, are only partially open to pressures of any kind. Practically all congressmen, and probably most state legislators, vote for bills in accord with their own personal convictions—when they have convictions with regard to specific bills—most of the time. Where they do not have convictions regarding a specific bill, the most important influence on them are the caucus leaders or committee chairmen of their own political party who are representing the party leadership's position. The "personal convictions" factor suggests that the *initial* selection of candidates and the means which they use to get elected to Congress are the two most important links in the chain leading to the passage of bills where influence can be most effectively applied. It is for this reason that we say that voluntary campaign labor, participation in the grass-roots party (as voluntary association), and monetary campaign contributions are the most powerful instruments to influence a legislator (or probably any other elected official).

In sharper summary, the conclusions of this book—in contrast with those of Mills and Hunter—are that power structure of the United States is highly complex and diversified (rather than unitary and monolithic), that the political system is more or less democratic (with the glaring exception of the Negro's position until the 1960's), that in political processes the political elite is ascendant over and not subordinate to the economic elite, and that the political elite influences or controls the economic elite at least as much as the economic elite controls the political elite. To arrive at such conclusions we must in part have a contrast conception: What should the American political power structure be compared to? We believe that Mills has implicitly compared the existing American power structure to some populist or guild socialist ideal, which has never existed and which we believe could never exist considering basic sociological facts —such as the existence of culture, of the value of money to most people, etc. Our implicit comparison in this book has been to any known other society—past or present (with the possible exception of the contemporary Scandinavian countries). We do not say that the multi-influence hypothesis is entirely the fact, or that the United States is completely democratic; we simply say that such statements are more correct for the United States today than for any other society.

. . . We wish merely to repeat in conclusion the statement of the multi-influence hypothesis which has guided the studies reported in this book: Segments of the economic elite have violated democratic political and legal processes, with differing degrees of effort and success in the various periods of American history, but in no recent period could they correctly be said to have controlled the elected and appointed political authorities in large measure. The relationship between the economic elite and the political authorities has been a constantly varying one of strong influence, co-operation, division of labor, and conflict, with each group influencing the other in changing proportion to some extent, and each operating independently of the other to a large extent. Today there is significant political control and limitation of certain activities of the economic elite, and there are also some significant processes by which the economic elite use their wealth to help elect some political candidates and to influence other political authorities in ways which are not available to the average citizen. Further, neither the economic elite nor the political authorities are monolithic units which act with internal consensus and co-ordinated action with regard to each other (or probably in any other way): in fact, there are several economic elites, which only very rarely act as units within themselves and among themselves, and there are at least two (we prefer to think of them as four) political parties which have significantly differing programs with regard to their actions toward any economic elite and each of these parties has only a partial degree of internal cohesion.

The power structure of the United States is indeed so complex that this book only touches on certain aspects of it, rather than providing full empirical evidence for these aspects. We believe, however, that enough empirical documentation has been provided to give basic support to the multi-influence hypothesis as a general statement about what is true of the power structure of the United States.

Robert A. Dahl

A CRITIQUE OF THE RULING ELITE MODEL

In the following selection, Robert A. Dahl, political scientist at Yale University and author of *Who Governs?*, critically analyzes the ruling elite model. Dahl argues that the evidence examined and the criteria employed in past studies have failed to provide a valid test of the ruling elite hypothesis.

A GREAT many people seem to believe that "they" run things: the old families, the bankers, the City Hall machine, or the party boss behind the scene. This kind of view evidently has a powerful and many-sided appeal. It is simple, compelling, dramatic, "realistic." It gives one standing as an inside-dopester. For individuals with a strong strain of frustrated idealism, it has just the right touch of hard-boiled cynicism. Finally, the hypothesis has one very great advantage over many alternative explanations: It can be cast in a form that makes it virtually impossible to disprove.

Consider the last point for a moment. There is a type of quasi-metaphysical theory made up of what might be called an infinite regress of explanations. The ruling elite model *can* be interpreted in this way. If the overt leaders of a community do not appear to constitute a ruling elite, then the theory can be saved by arguing that behind the overt leaders there is a set of covert leaders who do. If subsequent evidence shows that this covert group does not make a ruling elite, then the theory can be saved by arguing that behind the first covert group there is another, and so on.

Now whatever else it may be, a theory that cannot even in principle be controverted by empirical evidence is not a scientific theory. The least that we can demand of any ruling elite theory that purports to be more than a metaphysical or polemical doctrine is, first, that the burden of proof be on the proponents of the theory and not on its critics; and,

second, that there be clear criteria according to which the theory could be disproved.

With these points in mind, I shall proceed in two stages. First, I shall try to clarify the meaning of the concept "ruling elite" by describing a very simple form of what I conceive to be a ruling elite system. Second, I shall indicate what would be required in principle as a simple but satisfactory test of any hypothesis asserting that a particular political system is, in fact, a ruling elite system. Finally, I shall deal with some objections.

I. A SIMPLE RULING ELITE SYSTEM

If a ruling elite hypothesis says anything, surely it asserts that within some specific political system there exists a group of people who to some degree exercise power or influence over other actors in the system. I shall make the following assumptions about power:

1. In order to compare the relative influence of two actors (these may be individuals, groups, classes, parties, or what not), it is necessary to state the scope of the responses upon which the actors have an effect. The statement, "A has more power than B," is so ambiguous as to verge on the meaningless, since it does not specify the scope.

2. One cannot compare the relative influence of two actors who always perform identical actions with respect to the group influenced. What this means as a practical matter is that ordinarily one can test for differences in influence only

From "A Critique of the Ruling Elite Model," by Robert A. Dahl, *American Political Science Review*, LII (June, 1958), 463–469. Reprinted by permission of Robert A. Dahl and The American Political Science Association.

where there are cases of differences in initial preferences. At one extreme, the difference may mean that one group prefers alternative A and another group prefers B, A and B being mutually exclusive. At the other extreme, it may mean that one group prefers alternative A to other alternatives, and another group is indifferent. If a political system displayed complete consensus at all times, we should find it impossible to construct a satisfactory direct test of the hypothesis that it was a ruling elite system, although indirect and rather unsatisfactory tests might be devised.

Consequently, to know whether or not we have a ruling elite, we must have a political system in which there is a difference in preferences, from time to time, among the individual human beings in the system. Suppose, now, that among these individuals there is a set whose preferences regularly prevail in all cases of disagreement, or at least in all cases of disagreement over key political issues (a term I propose to leave undefined here). Let me call such a set of individuals a "controlling group." In a full-fledged democracy operating strictly according to majority rule, the majority would constitute a controlling group, even though the individual members of the majority might change from one issue to the next. But since our model is to represent a ruling elite system, we require that the set be *less than a majority in size*.

However, in any representative system with single member voting districts where more than two candidates receive votes, a candidate *could* win with less than a majority of votes; and it is possible, therefore, to imagine a truly sovereign legislature elected under the strictest "democratic" rules that was nonetheless governed by a legislative majority representing the first preferences of a minority of voters. Yet I do not think we would want to call such a political system a ruling elite system. Because of this kind of difficulty, I propose that we exclude from our definition of a ruling elite any controlling group that is a product of rules that are actually followed (that is, "real" rules) under which

a majority of individuals could dominate if they took certain actions permissible under the "real" rules. In short, to constitute a ruling elite a controlling group must not be *a pure artifact of democratic rules*.

A ruling elite, then, is a controlling group less than a majority in size that is not a pure artifact of democratic rules. It is a minority of individuals whose preferences regularly prevail in cases of differences in preference on key political issues. If we are to avoid an infinite regress of explanations, the composition of the ruling elite must be more or less definitely specified.

II. SOME BAD TESTS

The hypothesis we are dealing with would run along these lines: "Such and such a political system (the U.S., the U.S.S.R., New Haven, or the like) is a ruling elite system in which the ruling elite has the following membership." Membership would then be specified by name, position, socio-economic class, socio-economic roles, or what not.

Let me now turn to the problem of testing a hypothesis of this sort, and begin by indicating a few tests that are sometimes mistakenly taken as adequate.

The first improper test confuses a ruling elite with a group that has a high *potential for control*. Let me explain. Suppose a set of individuals in a political system has the following property: there is a very high probability that if they agree on a key political alternative, and if they all act in some specified way, then that alternative will be chosen. We may say of such a group, that it has a *high potential for control*. In a large and complex society like ours, there may be many such groups. For example, the bureaucratic triumvirate of Professor Mills would appear to have a high potential for control. In the City of New Haven, with which I have some acquaintance, I do not doubt that the leading business figures together with the leaders of both political parties have a high potential for control. But a potential for control is not, except in a peculiarly Hobbesian world, equivalent to actual control. If the military leaders of this country and their subordinates agreed that it was desirable, they could most assuredly establish a military dictatorship of the most overt sort; nor would they need the aid of leaders of business corporations or the executive branch of our government. But they have not set up such a dictatorship. For what is lacking are the premises I mentioned earlier, namely agreement on a key political alternative and some set of specific implementing actions. That is to say, a group may have a high potential for control and a *low potential for unity*. The actual *political effectiveness* of a group is a function of its potential for control *and* its potential for unity. Thus a group with a relatively low potential for control but a high potential for unity may be more politically effective than a group with a high potential for control but a low potential for unity.

The second improper test confuses a ruling elite with a group of individuals who have more influence than any others in the system. I take it for granted that in every human organization some individuals have more influence over key decisions than do others. Political equality may well be among the most Utopian of all human goals. But it is fallacious to assume that the absence of political equality proves the existence of a ruling elite.

The third improper test, which is closely related to the preceding one, is to generalize from a single scope of influence. Neither logically nor empirically does it follow that a group with a high degree of influence over one scope will necessarily have a high degree of influence over another scope within the same system. This is a matter to be determined empirically. Any investigation that does not take into account the possibility that different elite groups have different scopes is suspect. By means of sloppy questions one could easily seem to discover that there exists a unified ruling elite in New Haven; for there is no doubt that small groups of people make many key decisions. It appears to be the case, however, that the small group that runs urban redevelopment is not the same as the small group that runs public education, and neither is quite the same as the two small groups that run the two par-

ties. Moreover the small group that runs urban redevelopment with a high degree of unity would almost certainly disintegrate if its activities were extended to either education or the two political parties.

III. A PROPOSED TEST

If tests like these are not valid, what can we properly require?

Let us take the simplest possible situation. Assume that there have been some number—I will not say how many—of cases where there has been disagreement within the political system on key political choices. Assume further that the hypothetical ruling elite prefers one alternative and other actors in the system prefer other alternatives. Then unless it is true that in all or very nearly all of these cases the alternative preferred by the ruling elite is actually adopted, the hypothesis (that the system is dominated by the specified ruling elite) is clearly false.

I do not want to pretend either that the research necessary to such a test is at all easy to carry out or that community life lends itself conveniently to strict interpretation according to the requirements of the test. *But I do not see how anyone can suppose that he has established the dominance of a specific group in a community or a nation without basing his analysis on the careful examination of a series of concrete decisions.* And these decisions must either constitute the universe or a fair sample from the universe of key political decisions taken in the political system.

Now it is a remarkable and indeed astounding fact that neither Professor Mills nor Professor Hunter has seriously attempted to examine an array of specific cases to test his major hypothesis. Yet I suppose these two works more than any others in the social sciences of the last few years have sought to interpret complex political systems essentially as instances of a ruling elite.

To sum up: The hypothesis of the existence of a ruling elite can be strictly tested only if:

1. The hypothetical ruling elite is a well-defined group.
2. There is a fair sample of cases in-

volving key political decisions in which the preferences of the hypothetical ruling elite run counter to those of any other likely group that might be suggested.

3. In such cases, the preferences of the elite regularly prevail.

IV. DIFFICULTIES AND OBJECTIONS

Several objections might be raised against the test I propose.

First, one might argue that the test is *too weak*. The argument would run as follows: If a ruling elite *doesn't* exist in a community, then the test is satisfactory; that is, if every hypothetical ruling elite is compared with alternative control groups, and in fact no ruling elite exists, then the test will indeed show that there is no minority whose preferences regularly prevail on key political alternatives. But—it might be said—suppose a ruling elite *does* exist. The test will not *necessarily* demonstrate its existence, since we may not have selected the right group as our hypothetical ruling elite. Now this objection is valid; but it suggests the point I made at the outset about the possibility of an infinite regress of explanations. Unless we use the test on every possible combination of individuals in the community, we cannot be certain that there is not some combination that constitutes a ruling elite. But since there is no more *a priori* reason to assume that a ruling elite does exist than to assume that one does not exist, the burden of proof does not rest upon the critic of the hypothesis, but upon its proponent. And a proponent must specify what group he has in mind as his ruling elite. Once the group is specified, then the test I have suggested is, at least in principle, valid.

Second, one could object that the test is *too strong*. For suppose that the members of the "ruled" group are indifferent as to the outcome of various political alternatives. Surely (one could argue) if there is another group that regularly gets its way in the face of this indifference, it is in fact the ruling group in the society. Now my reasons for wishing to discriminate this case from the other involve more than a mere question of the propriety of using the term "ruling elite," which is only a term of convenience.

There is, I think, a difference of some theoretical significance between a system in which a small group dominates over another that is opposed to it, and one in which a group dominates over an indifferent mass. In the second case, the alternatives at stake can hardly be regarded as "key political issues" if we assume the point of view of the indifferent mass; whereas in the first case it is reasonable to say that the alternatives involve a key political issue from the standpoint of both groups. Earlier I refrained from defining the concept "key political issues." If we were to do so at this point, it would seem reasonable to require as a necessary although possibly not a sufficient condition that the issue should involve actual disagreement in preferences among two or more groups. In short, the case of "indifference vs. preference" would be ruled out.

However, I do not mean to dispose of the problem simply by definition. The point is to make sure that the two systems are distinguished. The test for the second, weaker system of elite rule would then be merely a modification of the test proposed for the first and more stringent case. It would again require an examination of a series of cases showing uniformly that when "the word" was authoritatively passed down from the designated elite, the hitherto indifferent majority fell into ready compliance with an alternative that had nothing else to recommend it intrinsically.

Third, one might argue that the test will not discriminate between a true ruling elite and a ruling elite together with its satellites. This objection is in one sense true and in one sense false. It is true that on a series of key political questions, an apparently unified group might prevail who would, according to our test, thereby constitute a ruling elite. Yet an inner core might actually make the decisions for the whole group.

However, one of two possibilities must be true. Either the inner core and the front men always agree at all times in the decision process, or they do not. But if they always agree, then it follows from one of our two assumptions about influence that the distinction between an "inner core" and "front men" has no operational meaning; that is, there is no conceivable way to distinguish between them. And if they do not always agree, then the test simply requires a comparison at those points in time when they disagree. Here again, the advantages of concrete cases are palpable, for these enable one to discover who initiates or vetoes and who merely complies.

Fourth, it might be said that the test is either too demanding or else it is too arbitrary. If it requires that the hypothetical elite prevails in *every single case*, then it demands too much. But if it does not require this much, then at what point can a ruling elite be said to exist? When it prevails in 7 cases out of 10? 8 out of 10? 9 out of 10? Or what? There are two answers to this objection. On the one hand, it would be quite reasonable to argue, I think, that since we are considering only key political choices and not trivial decisions, if the elite does not prevail in *every* case in which it disagrees with a contrary group, it cannot properly be called a ruling elite. But since I have not supplied an independent definition of the term "key political choices," I must admit that this answer is not wholly satisfactory. On the other hand, I would be inclined to suggest that in this instance as in many others we ought not to assume that political reality will be as discrete and discontinuous as the concepts we find convenient to employ. We can say that a system approximates a true ruling elite system, to a greater or lesser degree, without insisting that it exemplify the extreme and limiting case.

Fifth, it might be objected that the test I have proposed would not work in the most obvious of all cases of ruling elites, namely in the totalitarian dictatorships. For the control of the elite over the expression of opinion is so great that overtly there is no disagreement; hence no cases on which to base a judgment arise. This objection is a fair one. But we are not concerned here with totalitarian systems. We are concerned with the application of the techniques of modern investigation to American communities, where, except in vary rare cases, terror is not so pervasive that the investigator

is barred from discovering the preferences of citizens. Even in Little Rock, for example, newspaper men seemed to have had little difficulty in finding diverse opinions; and a northern political scientist of my acquaintance has managed to complete a large number of productive interviews with White and Negro Southerners on the touchy subject of integration.

Finally one could argue that even in a society like ours a ruling elite might be so influential over ideas, attitudes, and opinions that a kind of false consensus will exist—not the phony consensus of a terroristic totalitarian dictatorship but the manipulated and superficially self-imposed adherence to the norms and goals of the elite by broad sections of a community. A good deal of Professor Mills' argument can be interpreted in this way, although it is not clear to me whether this is what he means to rest his case on.

Even more than the others this objection points to the need to be circumspect in interpreting the evidence. Yet here, too, it seems to me that the hypothesis cannot be satisfactorily confirmed without something equivalent to the test I have proposed. For once again either the consensus is perpetual and unbreakable, in which case there is no conceivable way of determining who is ruler and who is ruled. Or it is not. But if it is not, then there is some point in the process of forming opinions at which the one group will be seen to initiate and veto, while the rest merely respond. And we can only discover these points *by an examination of a series of concrete cases where key decisions are made:* decisions on taxation and expenditures, subsidies, welfare programs, military policy, and so on.

It would be interesting to know, for example, whether the initiation and veto of alternatives having to do with our missile program would confirm Professor Mills' hypothesis, or indeed any reasonable hypothesis about the existence of a ruling elite. To the superficial observer it would scarcely appear that the military itself is a homogeneous group, to say nothing of their supposed coalition with corporate and political executives. If the military alone or the coalition together is a ruling elite, it is either incredibly incompetent in administering its own fundamental affairs or else it is unconcerned with the success of its policies to a degree that I find astounding.

However I do not mean to examine the evidence here. For the whole point of this paper is that the evidence for a ruling elite, either in the United States or in any specific community, has not yet been properly examined so far as I know. And the evidence has not been properly examined, I have tried to argue, because the examination has not employed satisfactory criteria to determine what constitutes a fair test of the basic hypothesis.

II. SOCIAL STRATIFICATION AND POWER

G. William Domhoff

THE AMERICAN GOVERNING CLASS

Differing interpretations of the nature of power and decision-making frequently involve disputes over the validity of assumptions and methodology. In the selection below from *Who Rules America?*, psychologist G. William Domhoff defends the sociology-of-leadership method as a research tool, a technique which concentrates on the sociological backgrounds of institutional leaders.

BEFORE looking at the term "governing class" in detail, it might be well to see how various theorists view the problem of power in the United States. For pluralists, the upper class is *no longer* a "ruling class." They argue that the upper class has lost its power over the past 30 or 35 years to a variety of "interest groups" or "veto groups" who contend for power on an almost equal footing. These veto groups include corporate managers (usually conceived of as a group apart from hereditary owners), technical-intellectual elites, organized farmers, organized laborers, consumers, and a strong federal government which has gained considerable autonomy from big business. . . .

On the other side of the fence from the pluralists are the Tocquevillian conservatives and the Marxist radicals. Both believe that the upper class remains an establishment or ruling class. Baltzell, speaking for the Tocquevillians, stresses the rise of a more ethnically representative establishment, while Sweezy stresses the increased importance of corporate executives at the expense of financiers. Standing between the pluralists and the ruling-class theorists are those who agree with C. Wright Mills. Mills was not impressed with the idea of distinguishing corporate executives from the hereditary

rich who make up the national upper class. He lumped owners and managers together as "the corporate rich." However, Mills believed that the Depression, World War II, and the Cold War brought leading politicians and generals to the top levels of power. The importance of these two groups led Mills to say that the corporate rich are no longer a ruling class but, at best, first among equals in a power elite. His theoretical model is closer to the pluralists in abandoning a ruling-class model, closer to the ruling-class model in stressing the unequal power of a trio of closely knit veto groups.

There are few empirically testable definitions of "ruling class" or "governing class." Bell speaks of a power-holding group with a "continuity of interests" and "community of interests," but like so many others, he does not stress what they must hold power over to qualify as a "ruling class." The definition given by Greer and Orleans at the start of this chapter stresses that the leaders holding command posts come from a hereditary social class with common norms and sanctions. Dahl presents the following definition of a ruling elite:

A ruling elite, then, is a controlling group less than a majority in size that is not a

G. William Domhoff, *Who Rules America?*, 141–153, 156, © 1967. Reprinted by permission of Prentice-Hall, Inc. Englewood Cliffs, New Jersey.

pure artifact of democratic rules. It is a minority of individuals whose preferences regularly prevail in cases of differences in preference on key political issues. If we are to avoid an infinite regress of explanations, the composition of the ruling elite must be more or less definitely specified.[1]

While Dahl's definition is valuable to us because it stresses that a ruling group must prevail on key political issues, it concerns a ruling-elite model, which is not quite the same as a governing-class model. A ruling-elite model implies that the same persons control a wide variety of issues, while a governing-class model implies only that the leaders are drawn from an upper class. There may or may not be more than one "ruling clique" within the "governing class," and as a matter of empirical fact, as has been shown, there are contending cliques within the American upper class of today. (Sometimes the cliques do not contend, but merely divide the labor.)

With the above definitions and the problems they imply uppermost in our minds, we developed the minimum definition of a "governing class" stated in the first chapter:

A governing class is a social upper class which receives a disproportionate amount of a country's income, owns a disproportionate amount of a country's wealth, and contributes a disproportionate number of its members to the controlling institutions and key decision-making groups in that country. . . .

THE SOCIOLOGY-OF-LEADERSHIP METHOD

The definition of a governing class that we have given is closely related to the method we have used in our study, namely, the "sociology-of-leadership" method. This method studies the social backgrounds of the men who control institutions and make decisions. It has two drawbacks. The first is that it does not demonstrate "consequences" from upper-class control. Do upper-class leaders have "special interests"? Donald Matthews, in *The Social Background of Political Decision-Makers*, warns that even

though most political leaders come from the higher social strata, they are not necessarily members of a "ruling class." . . .

It is misleading to assume that a group must literally be represented among the political decision-makers to have influence or political power. The unrepresentative nature of America's political decision-makers no doubt has its consequences, but it does not free them from their ultimate accountability to the electorate at large. Thus the frequency with which members of certain groups are found among decision-makers should not be considered an infallible index of the distribution of power in a society. In America at least lower-status groups have political power far in excess of their number in Congress, the Cabinet, and so on.

While this may sound farfetched, it is nonetheless plausible that the "real power" is in the masses, who let members of the upper class have the seats of honor as long as they make wise decisions. However, according to Dahl, this type of argument is usually used by ruling-class theorists who have not been able to find any members of the upper class in ruling positions.

The second problem with the sociology-of-leadership methodology is to determine how much overrepresentation is necessary to support the hypothesis that the upper class is a governing class. If all the leaders were from the upper class, there would be little objection to this method. Dahl, for example, used it to conclude that aristocrats used to control New Haven. But not all present-day leaders are from the upper class. How significant is it that a social group which would contribute 0.5 percent of the leaders in a completely open social system in fact contributes 100 or more times that number? Statistically speaking, the findings are "significant." But statistical significance is not everything. When does the difference really make a difference? It could be argued that this overrepresentation does not have the consequences implied. Perhaps the non-upper-class leaders have the power, if not the wealth. We have tried to deal with this second objection by understanding the backgrounds and training of the non-upper-class leaders. We have

[1] "A Critique of the Ruling Elite Model," *American Political Science Review*, LII, 1958, 464.

found in most instances that they were selected, trained, and employed in institutions which function to the benefit of members of the upper class and which are controlled by members of the upper class. From this we have argued that they are selected for advancement in terms of the interests of members of the upper class. We have thus introduced the "power elite" concept, which refers to high-level officials in institutions controlled by members of the upper class. We have emphasized that members of the power elite may or may not be members of the upper class, but that the power elite is rooted in the upper class and serves the interests of members of the upper class.

The weaknesses of the sociology-of-leadership method are not present in the study of the political decision-making process that is advocated by Dahl. However, this method has its own limitations. The first comment to be made on this approach is that it is concerned only with key political issues. Unless the word "political" is given broad definition, such a limitation may be unjustified—economic, educational, and cultural decisions may be equally important from the point of view of members of the governing class, because such decisions determine the framework within which political decisions are made. However, this is a minor objection. The first real problem is in determining what are the "key political issues." Is it fair, for example, to expect members of the upper class to be interested in local politics, when it is known that these issues do not really concern them? Again, the problem is not insurmountable. Dahl has offered an excellent list of issues in an offhand fashion by way of example—"taxation and expenditures, subsidies, welfare programs, military policy. . . ."[2] If it could be shown that these casual suggestions are the ones that would be settled upon by lengthy deliberations, a governing-class theorist would be nine-tenths of the way home in an attempt to support his hypothesis by the decision-making method. Members of the upper class and

their corporations benefit most from the tax structure and tax loopholes, large businesses receive most of the subsidies, welfare spending has dropped from $30 per citizen in 1939 when it made up 44 percent of the budget to $16 per citizen in 1963 when it made up 7 percent of the budget, and a group of *Social Register* listees and corporation executives make the key decisions on military policy.

A second objection to Dahl's concept of the decision-making method is that it gives little importance to the situation where one group prevails over indifferent groups. Dahl emphasizes this because there is "a difference of some theoretical significance between a system in which a small group dominates over another that is opposed to it, and one in which a group dominates over an indifferent mass."[3] This is certainly true, but the difference in *systems* is not at issue. It may be that there are ruling elites or ruling classes in many different types of systems, and that they would use different techniques of control in the different systems. A third major objection to the decision-making method is that it is very difficult to find the "real interests" of the various groups that may be involved in a decision. Or it may be many years before such interests can be determined, just as it may be many years before it can be determined whether or not the "outcome" favored one group or another. Closely related to this objection is the fact that it is often difficult to determine what factors are involved in the making of any given decision. Many aspects of a situation may remain secret or be forgotten or repressed, and the participants themselves may not be able to assess correctly the roles of the various members of the group. Dahl agrees that such a determination is "enormously difficult." We would stress that this is especially the case with corporations, the CIA, and the federal government, where a great deal of secrecy is the standard situation.

The final major difficulty with the decision-making model is that it does not specify how many decisions must be de-

[2] *Ibid.,* 469.   [3] *Ibid.,* 467.

cided in favor of the upper class. Can members of the upper class occasionally lose, or make concessions, and still be considered part of a governing class? This is analogous to the problem of how much overrepresentation is necessary with the sociology-of-leadership methodology. Dahl offers a solution when he says: "We can say that a system approximates a true ruling elite system, to a greater or lesser degree, without insisting that it exemplify the extreme and limiting case."[4] In short, an upper class can be more or less a governing class depending upon how many decisions it controls.

The differences between the sociology-of-leadership method and the decision-making method can be summarized as follows: The decision-making approach is concerned with issues and attempts to study the decision-making process and its outcome. The sociology-of-leadership methodology is concerned with sociological background and studies the sociological composition of institutional leadership and of decision-making groups. The decision-making method has trouble specifying key political issues, the real interests of the protagonists, the factors involved in the decision, and the long-run consequences of the outcome; the sociology-of-leadership method runs into trouble demonstrating that upper-class leaders have special interests and specifying how many of the decision-makers and institutional leaders must be members of the upper class. Recognizing the limitations of both methods, and of any and all methods, for that matter, we have chosen to emphasize the sociology-of-leadership method for the following reasons:

1. There is more agreement about the major institutions of American society than about the true interests of various socioeconomic groups.

2. It is possible to determine the sociological composition of a leadership group, but it is seldom possible to know all the factors and arguments that went into a decision, much less who initiated and vetoed specific proposals. This is especially the case when decisions are made in complete privacy, such as corporate board meetings, National Security Council meetings, and Special Group meetings.

3. It is possible to determine in a short time whether or not the decision-makers are members of a given socioeconomic class or employees of a given institution, but it is seldom possible to determine immediately what will be the effect of a given decision; this is necessary to determine which group was favored by the decision.

4. In a governing-class study, as opposed to a ruling-elite study, it is ultimately necessary to determine social class membership to determine whether or not the opposing elites or political parties are from the same or different social classes.

5. It is possible to partially answer the objection to the sociology-of-leadership method concerning the special interests of upper-class leaders by showing that members of the upper class own a disproportionate amount of the country's wealth, particularly corporate wealth, and receive a disproportionate amount of the yearly income.

EMPIRICAL OBJECTIONS

So much, then, for the problems of definition and methodology. We have moved from a definition of "social class" to the fact of a "national upper class" to a definition of "governing class" and "power elite," and we have given our reasons for emphasizing the sociology-of-leadership methodology in attempting to test our hypothesis. Our next step is to anticipate objections. This can be accomplished from our detailed study of criticisms of *The Power Elite.*

Scope and Magnitude of Power

The first question to be asked of a study emphasizing the sociology-of-leadership methodology concerns the specific powers that go with the various institutional positions held by members or representatives of the American upper class. Hacker points out that several of Mills's critics raised such a question about *The Power Elite.* Dahl emphasizes that a study such as ours must, among other

[4] *Ibid.,* 468.

things, demonstrate the basis, technique, scope, and magnitude of the power of the hypothetical ruling group. Our answer is as follows:

1. *The corporations*. The corporations are controlled by boards of directors. These boards have the final say-so on investment decisions. They can therefore influence the rate of national economic growth, the rise and fall of the stock market, and the number and type of jobs available. The corporate boards also choose the chief officers of the corporations, who in turn determine day-to-day operations and the advancement of lower-level managers. Dahl, relying primarily upon a study by Gordon, would dispute these statements. He believes that managers control the corporations, telling the directors which officers to advance to the very highest positions. Gordon, in turn, makes his claim because (a) 35 of 155 corporations had more "inside" than "outside" directors; (b) directors hold very little stock; and (c) the importance of interest groups has waned. We do not agree with Gordon's analysis for a number of reasons. First, we are inclined to accept the testimony of observers such as Berle who are closer to the day-to-day functioning of the corporate world. Second, the small amount of stock held by directors may be explained in other ways, such as its being held by one's wife or a bank trust. Third, the greater number of inside directors in some corporations is not necessarily significant. We have seen, for example, that many private school graduates go to work in the corporate world and on Wall Street. Also, inside directors are not necessarily indicative of management control. Family-owned companies, which are dominated by a few persons, often have many employees on the board. Fourth, where the evidence is available, as in the case of the Cleveland interest group, the Mellon interest group, and the du Pont interest group, there is no reason to believe that the power of interest groups has declined. Finally, we mean by "control" the power to change management if the operation of the corporation does not suit its owners. That managers make day-to-day business decisions on technical matters is really irrelevant.

As corporate spokesman after corporate spokesman makes clear, the primary goal is to make a profit, and that is what most concerns members of the upper class when it comes to their corporations.

2. *The corporation lawyers*. Corporate lawyers derive their power from their relationship to the corporate economy they helped to construct. They have the power of expertise on legal matters. They also have the power of persons who have a broader perspective of the system and can thereby give advice to those who function in narrower channels.

3. *The foundation boards*. The foundation boards have the power to accept or reject various scientific, educational, and cultural ventures. They therefore have the power to exert considerable influence over the noneconomic aspects of American life.

4. *The associations (CFR, FPA, BAC, CED, NAC, and NAM)*. The leaders of these associations, through their publications, seminars, and advertisements, have the power to influence public opinion. They also serve to educate persons who are going to be decision-makers in a given issue-area, such as economic development or foreign policy.

5. *The boards of trustees of universities*. The boards of trustees make long-term policy, thus setting the tone and orientation of the university. They also have the power to hire and fire university presidents and other top-level personnel.

6. *The Executive branch of the federal government*. The Executive branch takes the initiative in matters of legislation and federal spending. It includes departments such as State, Treasury, and Defense which control the crucial issue-areas of foreign policy, financial policy, and military policy. The Executive branch also has appointive powers over the Judicial branch and the independent regulatory agencies. It can use its prestige to influence public opinion and its expertise to influence Congress.

7. *The military*. The military has the power to carry out whatever activity is called for by the National Security Council and the Defense Department. It has the power of expertise in giving advice

on whether or not to undertake a given operation, how various operations should be carried out, and which branches of the military should be utilized in defense planning and military operations. Once a plan has been set, the military has the power to decide on operational details and to select personnel to carry out the task. The military has the power to influence public opinion through its large public relations apparatus.

The Managerial Revolution

The second major objection likely to be raised has to do with the decline of family capitalism and the rise of the managers (the managerial revolution). It is often argued that the owners no longer control and that the managers are a separate social group from the social upper class of stockholders. Sometimes it is argued that the rich have been diminished by inheritance taxes. Contrary to these arguments, it has been shown that successful managers become owners themselves with the help of stock options and stock tips, and that they are assimilated socially into the upper class. It also has been shown that a considerable number of corporate executives are of the upper class originally even when they are not majority owners in a given corporation. Finally, it has been shown that stock ownership is not so dispersed that it is meaningless. The rich have *not* lost in wealth, and may even be gaining because of easily avoided taxes. On the basis of these findings, it has been argued that the dispersal of stock ownership within the upper class makes members of this class concerned with the success of the system as a whole rather than with their own given company, as was the case with family capitalism. It was further argued that the dispersal of stock and the death of family capitalism freed the hereditary rich to go into government service, the professions, and the arts, contributing further to their control of the system and to its stability.

The Role of Expertise

A third major objection has to do with the importance of expertise in the modern world and the rise of the "meritocracy." This argument, which incorporates the rise of the corporate managers as one of its examples, claims that the upper-middle class of well-educated specialists, who are drawn before their training from all socioeconomic levels, has replaced the upper class of property owners as the wielders of power, as the makers of big decisions. There are several comments that can be made about this argument:

1. To advise a decision-maker is not to make a decision. As Mills was well aware, experts are often the "captains" of the power elite's higher thoughts, but as he also said of chief executives, "Theirs [is] the Judgment."[5] It is the function of the decision-maker to choose among the usually conflicting advice that he receives from his usually divided experts.

2. Final authority, or decision-making power, does not follow from the fact that one is necessary to the functioning of a system. Most parts of any system are necessary. It is perfectly possible for one part of a system to function for the benefit of another, which is the point we have argued by stressing the distribution of income and wealth.

3. We believe it is an *empirical* mistake to downgrade the amount of expertise located *within* the upper class. Too much is made of "café society," "the jet set," and the "functionless genteel" within the upper class. The fact is that most members of the upper class are hard-working and competent. We have demonstrated this in a number of ways:

a. Almost all graduates of private schools go on to college. Our study of one alumni bulletin showed that private school graduates go into a variety of activities that require a considerable amount of expertise.

b. Private school graduates go to the finest universities in the country, universities which are the major suppliers of American expertise.

c. Our study of the 1965 *Social Register Locater* showed that 8 percent of a sample of 182 adult males have the title "doctor" before their names. Whether the degree is medical or academic, this percentage suggests a considerable amount of expertise within the upper class. Balt-

[5] *The Power Elite*, 1956, 136.

zell's study of Philadelphia suggests the same for medicine and architecture in that city.

d. Baltzell's study showed that one-fourth of the *Who's Who* listees from *Social Register* cities were in the *Social Register*.

e. Almost one third of the partners in the largest Wall Street law firms, a major source of American legal and political expertise, are listed in the *Social Register*. Baltzell's study of Philadelphia revealed several upper-class law firms in that city.

4. The major producers of expertise —*e.g.*, Harvard, Yale, Princeton, Columbia, Penn, and Stanford—are controlled by members of the American upper class. This implies at the very least the power to select and train those who will be experts.

5. Military experts are selected by the Department of Defense, which is dominated by members of the upper class and by high-level corporate executives.

6. Experts are advanced and acclaimed in accordance with their success in solving problems posed by a system which disproportionately benefits members of the upper class.

For all of these reasons, we do not believe that experts from the middle class have somehow displaced the American upper class as a governing class. They are well rewarded for their services to this group, however.

Conflict Within the Upper Class

Do the disagreements within the upper class contradict the notion that it is a governing class? Is such disagreement evidence for a pluralistic model? The answer is that it is very possible for members of a governing class to disagree as to what long-range strategies should be, not to mention short-range tactics. . . . Nor is the day-to-day reality of conflict, as depicted so beautifully in the case of the federal government by Cater in *Power in Washington*, necessarily in conflict with a governing-class theory. Sweezy believes that the pluralistic model integrates "a considerable body of observed fact" in a "tolerably satisfactory fashion." However, he also believes that "the state has a function in society which

is prior to and more fundamental than any which present-day liberals attribute to it."[6] He is referring to the protection of private property as a system.

So What?

Another objection would run as follows. So what if the upper class controls a disproportionate amount of the wealth, and controls the corporations and the federal government? The important thing is whether or not their decisions are in the interests of the country as a whole. Would members of other classes make similar decisions on key issues? The answer to this question, above and beyond the special interests that are implied by disproportionate income and wealth, is that it is not really pertinent. This book has not tried to show that the rule of the American upper class has been a benevolent one or a malevolent one. Rather, it is concerned with the existence and the mechanics of the national upper class, not with an interpretation of the impact of its rule on American civilization for better or for worse. Whether decisions by members of the upper class are "good" for the whole country or only for themselves is difficult to answer in any case, but it is not relevant to the existence of a governing class by our definition. Such a criticism assumes that a study of social structure implies an attack on that social structure, but that is only the case, to quote Mills, under certain circumstances: "When little is known, or only trivial items publicized, or when myths prevail, then plain description becomes a radical fact—or at least is taken to be radically upsetting."[7]

Restraints

An objection closely related to the one immediately above could be formulated as follows. Even if it is true that one socioeconomic group owns a disproportionate share of the wealth and contributes a considerable percentage of national leaders, the fact remains that there are restraints on decision-makers. There

[6] *The Theory of Capitalist Development*, 1942, 240–241.
[7] "Comments on Criticism," *Dissent*, V, 1957, 33.

are opposing interest groups and opposing socioeconomic classes, such as workers, farmers, small businessmen, and consumers, and there are restraining cultural values, as manifested in the Constitution, the Bill of Rights, civil rights laws, and the golden rule. Most of all, there is the right to vote, which means that the leaders are accountable to all the people. After showing that blue-collar workers are almost totally excluded from decision-making roles in New Haven, Dahl points to their restraining powers:

Nonetheless, it would be wrong to conclude that the activities and attitudes of people in these strata have no influence on the decisions of governmental officials. Though wage earners lack social standing, they are not without other resources, including the ballot, and what they lack as individuals they more than make up in collective resources. In short, although their direct influence is low, their indirect collective influence is high.[8]

We would agree, in Dahl's terms, that the underlying population's "potential for control" is infinitely greater than that of the upper class, but we would add that the "potential for unity" is much greater in the latter than it is in the former, which is hopelessly divided into income classes, religious groups, ethnic groups, and racial groups. We also would agree that there are restraints on the power of the governing class, for the governing class is part of a system which includes other nation-states as well as other socioeconomic groups. We would even agree that members of the power elite often try to anticipate the reactions of other groups when they make their decisions. The potential power of angry, organized masses is well known in twentieth-century America thanks to foreign revolutions, the battle over women's suffrage, labor strikes, and the civil rights movement.

But Businessmen Hate Government

The final, and most important, objection that is usually raised against a governing-class model concerns the apparent autonomy of the federal government. Critics point to the New Deal, the Democratic Party, anti-business legislation, and the intense hostility of business to government in support of the idea that the federal government is a relatively autonomous institution that adjudicates disputes among various interest groups. Talcott Parsons finds business opposition to government "impossible to understand" unless we assume "genuine, and in some sense effective" governmental control of business.[9] Similarly, economist Edward S. Mason, an expert on corporations and a former president of the American Economic Association, was paraphrased as follows in *Business Week:* "Business' intense opposition to every proposed surrender of power to Washington is hardly consistent with the view that it itself dominates the U.S. government."[10]

In answer to these objections, this study has shown who controlled the New Deal—liberal elements of the American upper class, including many ex-Republicans. We have stressed that the New Deal created a split within the power elite which has not yet healed. Many members of the upper class remain unreconciled to the New Deal, believing that aristocrat Franklin Roosevelt ("Rosenfelt") was a traitor to his class who was part of an international Communist-Jewish conspiracy. However, this does not mean that other members of the upper class did not control the New Deal. As Baltzell documents, the New Deal was actually the beginning of a more ethnically representative establishment within the governing class which pushed aside the Protestant Establishment made up of heavy industrialists, fiscal conservatives, and prejudiced personalities. On a larger time scale, 1932–1964, this study has answered the claim that the federal government is autonomous by showing that the now-dominant Executive branch is honeycombed to an overwhelming degree by members of the power elite. This same evidence, buttressed by studies of campaign financing,

[8] Robert A. Dahl, *Who Governs?*, 1961, 229.

[9] Talcott Parsons, *Structure and Process in Modern Societies*, 1960, 213–214.
[10] *Business Week*, April 13, 1963.

also disposes of the myth that the Democratic Party is not controlled by elements of the American upper class. As to the charge that the upper class is not omnipotent, and therefore not a governing class, the fact remains that a very wealthy upper class which makes concessions remains a wealthy upper class. It stoops to conquer, taking the advice of its English counterparts rather than the foolhardy path of the French landlords.

*   *   *

Now the reader has been introduced to the main arguments raised in the past when the upper reaches of society have been studied with the sociology-of-leadership methodology. He must re-assess these arguments in the light of the empirical evidence presented in the previous chapters. For ourselves, we conclude that the income, wealth, and institutional leadership of what Baltzell calls the "American business aristocracy" are more than sufficient to earn it the designation "governing class." As Sweezy would say, this "ruling class" is based upon the national corporate economy and the institutions that economy nourishes. It manifests itself through what the late C. Wright Mills called the power elite.

Nelson W. Polsby

COMMUNITY POWER AND STRATIFICATION THEORY

In the selection which follows, political scientist Nelson W. Polsby questions the utilization of stratification theory in evaluating community power. Polsby argues that such studies have been characterized by forced evidence, a disregard for data contrary to the major hypotheses, and conclusions which fail to be justified by conditions in the communities under examination.

STRATIFICATION studies make five assertions in common about power in American communities.

The first proposition is:

1. *The upper class rules in local community life:* Stratification studies differ in their descriptions of what constitutes the upper class. Some divide the classes on economic grounds, others according to status ascriptions by community residents. Some authors divide communities into two classes, others into five or six classes. Some authors hold that classes are "real" categories which are understood by citizens of the community and are used in their daily lives; others aver that classes are not real but rather are constructs convenient for analysis. While these differences are important to the study of social stratification, they are side issues in the present context. *All* students of stratification agree that it is possible to talk about different classes in society. Although many assert that in principle communities can be stratified according to differences in the amount of power held by individuals, all stratify communities on some basis other than power. It is these other bases for stratification that will concern us for a moment. These include income, occupation, housing, social participation, consump-

From *Community Power And Political Theory* by Nelson W. Polsby, 8–11, 98–111. Copyright ©
1963 by Yale University. Reprinted by permission of Yale University Press.

tion patterns. All of these are considered indices of social or economic standing, so it is proper to refer to the "upper class" as a group in the community of highest social-economic standing, without prejudice to any of the many different ways in which stratification writers arrive at their identification of this group. It is possible to suggest another formulation of this proposition: The group with the highest social-economic standing has the most power. If we can think of a "base" of power as a condition necessary for the exercise of power, then we can state the proposition in still another way: a high social-economic position is the base of most community power.

Social stratification theory organizes individuals for analytical purposes into "strata," stacked one on the other. Thus stratification writers on community power see the upper class as at the top of a ladder of power, with others ranged below them. One of the most significant of the lower groups is composed of civic leaders and politicians, who are not themselves members of the upper class. Of these people, stratification writers assert:

2. *Political and civic leaders are subordinate to the upper class:*

Subordination in two senses is implied or asserted in stratification studies of community power. Political and civic leaders as a group are said to possess less power than the upper class as a group, and in addition (or perhaps as a consequence of having less power) they are held to take orders from or do the bidding of the upper class.

A third assertion of the stratification theory is:

3. *A single "power elite" rules in the community.*

This constitutes an extension and elaboration of the propositions already expressed. We may think of an elite as a small group, always less than a majority of the community, and as a group selected by some means other than majority vote. The upper class in every community studied fits these criteria. Another idea suggested by the term "power elite" is that the powers of the elite group are distributed over a large num-

ber of significant community decisions, so that stratification writers may say of the power elite that it stands at the apex of a pyramid of "all-purpose" power, dealing with a wide variety of community issues. This group is also held to be homogeneous in its social composition, being made up of members of the upper class.

Each of the various possible outcomes of issues may be said to allocate valued things and events in alternative ways. Stratification writers hold that it is in the interests of each class in society to increase its long-run share of values, but of course rulership implies that only one class possesses the means to accomplish this end. Hence the assertion of stratification writers that:

4. *The upper-class power elite rules in its own interests.*

This arrangement, according to stratification writers, is not or at least should not be acquiesced to willingly by the other classes in society. The final characteristic of community power asserted in stratification studies is therefore that:

5. *Social conflict takes place between the upper and lower classes.*

The reasoning here is that significant social conflicts follow the significant divisions of interest in the community, and these cleavages of interest separate the community's upper from its lower social classes rather than divide other groups in the community whose members are recruited on some basis other than class memberships.

*   *   *

Three possible explanations will be advanced for the fact that the political theory of so many students of community power led them seriously astray. One explanation is that their political tastes and preferences made them want to believe that the five key propositions were true of American communities, and they were therefore victims of their personal biases. Another explanation holds that the basic axioms and presuppositions of stratification theory are such that the five key propositions can be deduced logically from them, so that by accepting the basic axioms of stratification theory researchers were unwittingly led to accept the five propositions. A third line of argument, supplementary to the second, holds that researchers were deceived by the entire intellectual framework of stratification theory. This explanation suggests that, embedded in the literature of social stratification, there are criteria governing the applicability of stratification analysis to society, and, by violating these criteria, students of community power made it highly probable that their findings would be faulty.

Let us consider the third explanation first. We can treat stratification theory, in its broadest outline, as an intellectual perspective which views society as an organism analogous in its structure to a layer cake. Writers on social stratification discuss such matters as who belongs in what layer and why, what goes on in each layer, and what relations are like between people in different layers. Stratification itself refers to the distributions of values in society. The way in which these values are distributed is critical: inequalities must exist, and, more than that, must persist if we are to say that stratification has taken place in a social system. Let us examine the rules of stratification analysis implied in this characterization.

We can think of values as things or events desired by individuals and groups in society. The values most often employed in modern stratification analysis are variants of the following three: life chances, prestige, and power. It is asserted—and, where not asserted, implied —in stratification analysis that these three values are distributed unequally in society, that they can be quantified at least roughly by the observer, and that individuals, or at least "classes" of individuals, are ordered transitively with respect to their possession of each value, so that it can be said that if A has more of value X than B and B than C, then A has more of value X than C. This third step gives an element of the stability mentioned above; it is also presumed in stratification analysis that everyone in a nuclear family will enjoy the same value-position with respect to each value and that these value-positions will tend to be passed on from generation to generation in the same family.

These are presumptions about empirical reality, hence criteria are immediately available for judging the conditions under which stratification analysis is appropriate. That is, insofar as conditions in the real world actually approximate the characteristics imputed to them by stratification analysts, the discussion of interclass relations and the life-styles, behavior, and attitudes of individuals as members of social classes is meaningful. But insofar as this is not the case stratification analysis may lead to great errors in describing social reality.

Let us turn to the three commonest dimensions of stratification theory and discuss briefly their appropriateness as variables in an analysis of modern American society. We shall be asking of each variable in turn: (1) can it be quantified by an observer? (2) is it distributed unequally in society? (3) are individuals and groups ordered transitively with respect to it? (4) does everyone in the nuclear family enjoy the same amount of it? (5) is it passed on from generation to generation in the same family?

A recent text in social stratification says of life chances:

In modern industrial societies members of the same economic class have similar chances to obtain certain values and opportunities which are of primary importance for life and survival. "Everything from the chance to stay alive during the first year after birth to the chance to view fine arts, the chance to remain healthy and grow tall, and if sick to get well again quickly, the chance to avoid becoming a juvenile delinquent—and very crucially, the chance to complete an intermediary or higher educational grade"—all these *life chances* are crucially influenced by one's position in the economic class structure.[1]

The economic structure in turn refers to the amount and source of income:

Individuals of the same or similar economic position have identical or similar

[1] Kurt Mayer, *Class and Society*, Garden City, 1955, 23.

goods and services to offer in the system of production and distribution and therefore receive identical or similar monetary rewards in the market place.[2]

It is, of course, easy to quantify income amounts, and this is the baseline of economic stratification. The source of income is an ambiguous variable, used in conjunction with the first to make predictions (or inferences) about the consumption patterns of individuals and about how they spend their time, and these variables in turn are also subject to measurement. The fact that income *source* is called an economic variable, may, however, produce spurious correlations between the economic and status hierarchies.

There are additional problems in quantification. Some income is received in kind—traditionally in the form of home-grown produce, but more recently in the form of fringe benefits. The availability of tax-supported public services, e.g. public housing, free welfare clinics, and public libraries, also makes a difference in real income. There are, finally, regional differences in purchasing power and various forms of taxation having differential impacts, and they too must be taken into account in order to give a strictly accurate measure of an individual's comparative economic position. However, all of these obstacles can be overcome in principle, and a satisfactory quantification of economic positions can be achieved.

It is an easily defended proposition that wealth, and hence purchasable advantages of various kinds, is unequally distributed in society. That these unequal relations can be ordered transitively seems intuitively obvious. It is also obvious that, in normal circumstances, a wife and child enjoy life chances which correspond with those of the head of their household. Finally, wealth, therefore life chances, can pass through inheritance from generation to generation.

Much the same story can be told, with perhaps a few more reservations, of the distribution of social status in society.

The social status structure implies that there is a pattern of deference in society in which individuals recognize others as being "above" or "beneath" them, or "on the same level," for purposes of sociability. These inequalities are observed and quantified in a variety of ways: social scientists have recorded numerous sets of self-and-other ratings by individuals in communities, by panels of especially knowledgeable citizens, and by participant observers. Numerous objective criteria are used in the rating process by citizens themselves and by observers. These criteria have included: family background, residence location, occupation, education, social participations (kinds and numbers of social memberships), and "style of life," which subsumes patterns of consumption and adherence to various canons of "taste" and/or "fashion."

Congruence among these various measures of status is not always high, hence instabilities in status are not uncommon. This occasionally prevents a strict transitive status ordering of individuals. A may successfully claim deference from B and B from C in a small town, on account of superiority in family connections. But when they are placed in a metropolitan environment, their consumption patterns may reverse this order or possibly render the exchange of deference entirely unpredictable.

However, the status positions of many families in many communities are apparently relatively well fixed. The fact that this applies to entire families is deemed so well established as to preclude the necessity for empirical testing. In fact, it is generally well known that, while the breadwinner establishes the status of a family, it is his wife who enforces the maintenance of status boundaries and his children who perpetuate these arrangements through their social participations, the most important of which is the marriage market.

All of the foregoing is elementary doctrine of social stratification analysis, to be found in any textbook on the subject. It is mentioned only as an introduction to what should be a surprising observation: that the third famous dimension of

[2] *Ibid.*

stratification analysis, power, fits only one of the criteria of stratification analysis at all well. It is in no wise comparable to the variables class and status in its fit with the criteria of stratification analysis.

Let us consider the first criterion: is it possible for an observer, through empirical observations, to arrive at an estimate of who has more and who has less power? This has never been done in stratification studies except by definition. Thus C. Wright Mills *defines* as America's power elite those occupying specified positions in military, economic, and political hierarchies. Milton Gordon cites power as a dimension of social stratification, owing to the fact that power distributions are "inherently hierarchical." But we must reject the substitution of definition for observation because obviously a construct which exists in language need not exist in the real world, and the task of stratification analysis is to clarify man's social behavior, not to indulge in circularities.

Another attempt to satisfy the first criterion holds that power can be observed empirically, but suggests as evidence the identical observations which were used as indices of economic or status positions. As an example of this, Kurt B. Mayer says in his text:

We have defined power as the ability to control the behavior of others. Sociologically, power refers especially to the control which certain groups and individuals are able to exercise over the life chances of others.[3]

The difficulty with this formulation is that the "life chances" of an individual refers to the characteristic which defines his *economic* position, as we have seen. When one individual controls the life chances of another, this is usually an indication of his superior *economic* position (e.g. boss vs. employee). Thus "control over the life chances of others" is at best a highly ambiguous criterion for use as an index of the power of actors, and, at worst, the observations suggested

by this criterion are identical with those one would make to ascertain the economic class position or life chances of an individual. Others make an analogous mistake with respect to social status. As long as we adhere to the notion that power is an empirically separable variable of social stratification, we must reject these as improper, and search for specific, separate empirical indices by which power can be measured. Stratification analysis has so far failed to fulfill this criterion.

As for the second criterion, it seems intuitively obvious that power is distributed unequally in society. But this most basic of criteria merely invites us to state the shape and durability of the inequality.

The difficulty of making such a statement becomes plain when we attempt to satisfy the criterion of transitivity. Robert Dahl states the dilemma nicely:

With an average probability approaching one, I can induce each of 10 students to come to class for an examination on a Friday afternoon when they would otherwise prefer to make off for New York or Northampton. With its existing resources and techniques, the New Haven Police Department can prevent about half the students who park along the streets near my office from staying beyond the legal time limit. Which of us has the more power? The question is, I believe, incapable of being answered unless we are ready to treat my relationships with my students as in some sense comparable with the relations of the Police Department with another group of students. Otherwise any answer would be arbitrary, because there is no valid way of combining the three variables—scope, number of respondents and change in probabilities—into a single scale.[4]

The question of transitivity merely compounds the comparability problem outlined by Dahl. If there is no satisfying way of comparing A's power with B's, then how much less likely it is that we can arrive at some agreement with respect to all three relationships, A-B, B-C, and A-C!

As for the fourth criterion, Robert

---

[3] *Ibid.*, 26.

[4] Robert A. Dahl, "The Concept of Power," *Behavioral Science*, II (July, 1957), 206.

Schulze has urged that we regard power exercise as a relationship not merely between persons, but between persons occupying particular positions. Thus Professor Dahl's chances of seeing me in an examination on any hypothetical Friday declined precipitously when I completed his courses. This common-sense formulation of the power relation also reveals that the members of a power-holder's family seldom have anything to do with his power exercise, except insofar as they can influence the power-holder directly. Ellen Dahl's ability to detain one or several Yale students in New Haven should not be confused with the comparatively futile efforts her father might make in the same direction.

There are occasional examples in American history where the power of one member of a family was shared among members of his household. The activities of Mrs. Woodrow Wilson during her husband's sickness in office is perhaps the most striking case in point. But no one is likely to mistake an historical rarity for a social pattern.

The final criterion has to do with the inheritance of power by the children of the powerful. No one will deny that there is a tradition in American politics according to which certain families enter public service; several generations of these families have unquestionably been prominent in positions of power and public trust. One thinks, for example, of the Byrds of Virginia, the Longs of Louisiana, Lodges of Massachusetts, and Frelinghuysens of New Jersey. But additional facts must be kept in mind. These positions of public trust are not inherited as a matter of course, but rather must be achieved by some kind of personal accomplishment even by inheritors of a long family tradition of public service. Family background often provides extremely good opportunities for the sons of political notables to display their talents, but their personal accomplishments are by no means irrelevant to their subsequent rise to positions of power in their own right. This of course does not mean that political leaders from politically prominent families necessarily possess unusual competence at the tasks they

perform, since those qualities that may be necessary to achieve public office or political leadership—e.g. popularity—are not always useful in the day-to-day conduct of business. In any event, it should be noted that far from a majority of the powerful are children of the powerful, as can be seen by even a casual census of, let us say, current chief executives of American cities and states. And it is also obvious that only a minority of the offspring of the powerful go on to become politically notable themselves. This provides a vivid contrast with the dimensions of class and status, where, as a matter of course, children inherit the positions of their parents. The passage of power by inheritance alone in modern America, while it is not unheard of, is surely a deviant, not a dominant pattern.

If the argument is persuasive that modern American community life is a relatively inappropriate setting for the application of a stratification analysis, then it follows that those who try to make such an analysis run certain risks. The two characteristic pitfalls are similar to those confronting a man doing a jigsaw puzzle. On the one hand, he must not force pieces into places they do not fit. On the other, he must not have any odd pieces left over when he completes his work. As we have seen, stratification studies of community power have on occasion both forced their data and ignored contrary evidence. But this is understandable, since stratification analysis presumes the existence of stable, significant inequalities. Stratification writers have stated this as a finding, but in reality these inequalities are a *presumption* without which stratification analysis is impossible.

But why was stratification theory employed at all? A hypothesis worth exploring is that stratification theory somehow fits the policy preferences or the personal, emotional needs of researchers. This argument is hard to sustain if for no other reason than that stratification writers have in general eschewed direct expositions of their social and political values. In the three instances in which this has not been the case, however, there has been a disparity of views. C.

Wright Mills has indicated his distress at the pattern of dominance he detects in modern society, characterizing it as conducive to a "higher immorality." Digby Baltzell, on the other hand, celebrated the identical pattern in Philadelphia as a necessary check on the abuse of power by leaders unacculturated to upper-class *noblesse oblige*. The Lynds expressed great discontent at the low standards of administrative morality and efficiency which prevailed in Middletown as the result of the alleged withdrawal of the "better" people from political life, but they also decried the antidemocratic hegemony of the business class, thus placing themselves on both sides of the question.

We can say, then, that diametrically opposed policy positions are supported equally well by the stratification analysis of community power. The five key propositions can be deduced from the social values of neither Mills nor Baltzell. Nor can either set of values be deduced from their "findings" about power. It is possible that several researchers were led to the same false conclusion each for a different reason. But I am proceeding on the assumption that this was not the case and that a common source of error exists.

If the political views of researchers do not provide a suitable rationale for the employment of stratification theory, one may hypothesize that the intellectual framework of stratification theory was a natural one for sociologists to use. According to one prevailing opinion among sociologists, stratification theory was erroneously supposed by researchers to have been inappropriate for the study of American life until certain twentieth-century events—notably the depression —reawakened interest in the study of social inequality and in the Marxian prophecy of capitalist self-destruction. By the time most of the studies discussed in this book were written, stratification theory was enjoying great popularity, and it is not too much to say that today stratification analysis is one of the commonest, most conventional perspectives from which sociologists view social life.

I turn, finally, to certain basic presumptions, axioms, and definitions of stratification theory itself, for the light they may throw on the source of common error. The first hypothesis suggested reasons why the application of stratification theory might have been expected to produce errors in describing social reality. The present discussion attempts to discover why these particular errors, embodied in the five key propositions, were made.

Stratification means, of course, the division of the community into strata, or layers, one on top of the other. Each individual in the community can in principle be located in a layer, and no one is found in more than a single layer at any point in time. This suggests that by some criterion or other there is always an identifiable top layer in the community, whose members are more or less firmly fixed in place.

Power, in stratification theory, consists of the *capacity* to realize one's will, even over objections. The emphasis upon capacity is important, because it signifies the stratification writers' attempt to find some relatively unambiguous set of resources which unfailingly index this capacity successfully (i.e., which predict the outcomes of conflicts). As we saw earlier, stratification writers customarily fall back on the indices of high class or status position as indices of power. Given these presumptions, one might deduce the first proposition: the upper class rules because the upper class is at the top of the economic and status hierarchy, and capacity to realize one's will (or to rule or prevail in decision-making) is indexed by class and status position.

Another characteristic of stratification analysis is to blur the distinction between values accruing to an individual and those accruing to a group. This is a serious matter when collective activity is involved; less so when individuals deal directly with individuals. In the latter case, let us say that the middle class, with 40 percent of the nation's population, has $100 million in wealth, while the upper class, with 3 percent of the population, has $50 million. We would say, then, that the per capita wealth of the upper class was greater, but that the collective wealth of the middle class was greater. In assessing the life chances of an individual, it is clearly his per capita value position which is relevant, and not the aggregate value position of all the members of his class.

But in order to maintain the proposition that the upper class rules, stratification theory must make the assumption that per capita power is irrelevant. Rather, the power position of a class must be considered a collective property, and the upper class always must have more of the total amount of power in the community than any other group. Without this proviso, we could conceive of situations in which all the members of the more numerous lower classes got together and outvoted the upper class; hence, the upper class would not rule. The fact that this sometimes happens suggests one limitation on the utility of the assumption. But a more serious objection may be raised: how can the power of the class a man belongs to be revealed by his individual life chances? The set of logical leaps which by implication establishes the identity of individual and collective value-positions is an unfortunate aspect of stratification theory. Once accomplished, they enable us to observe that political and civic leaders are subordinate to economic and social leaders because the latter group occupies the top, and no matter how numerous or powerful civic leaders become they can never, by the rules of stratification analysis, collectively exceed the power of the upper class.

A single power elite is seen to rule in American community life because stratification theory provides for differentiation only between ranks in a hierarchy; hence those who belong to some group other than the top group are nonrulers, and all those who belong to the top group are rulers.

The interests of a group may be defined as maximizing its long-run share of values. In stratification theory, every group is presumed to be pursuing its own interests. Insofar as a group fails to do so, it is presumed to lack information and organization. The upper class is presumed to be uniquely endowed with information, organization, and all other conceivable means for pursuing rational activity, i.e., maximizing its long-run share of values. Therefore, the conclusion must be that the upper class rules in its own interests.

A final set of stratification theory presumptions has to do with the scarcity of values in society. This means that each class, in maximizing its own long-run share of values, runs up against other classes bent on the same end. Conflict takes place because values demanded exceed values supplied, and this scarcity sets off class conflict. Again, groups other than classes are not seen as conflicting for values because stratification theory differentiates clearly only between classes; other groups, lacking a place in the basic language of stratification analysis, are not unimportant so much as invisible.

The key propositions of the stratification analysis therefore follow from the basic axioms and definitions of stratification theory. It seems highly improbable that propositions different from those given would appear as findings in stratification studies, given the assumptions that (1) the community is divided horizontally, into ranked layers, with a single layer on top; (2) power is a collective attribute of classes indexed by the per capita economic and status value positions of class members; (3) classes are oriented to the goal of maximizing their long-run share of values; (4) the total supply of values in the community is smaller than the demands of the various classes. Since each of these conditions is postulated, explicitly or implicitly, in stratification theory, it seems legitimate to conclude that the key propositions could have been deduced from basic axioms. This may explain why stratification writers have advanced similar propositions about community power despite the fact that the propositions were not justified by the facts in the communities they studied.

III. THE CORPORATE STRUCTURE AND POWER

Gabriel Kolko

THE CONCENTRATION OF CORPORATE POWER

In the selection below from *Wealth And Power In America,* historian Gabriel Kolko attacks the commonly held assumption that American industry represents a democratic economic system. Rather than focusing on the use or abuse of power, involving interaction between the business community and society, Kolko concentrates on the actual ownership and control of America's largest corporations.

THE distribution of power over corporations, the dominant sector of the economy, is of major consequence in determining the extent to which America has attained a democratic economic structure.

Most recent theoretical discussions of the role of the corporation in American life have ignored the facts about the actual distribution of corporate power in favor of theories about the relationship of the corporation to the rest of society and the nature of the corporate executive as an individual.

The dominant image of the corporate leadership today is that of the responsible trustee. This concept has its roots in a basic proposition set forth by Berle and Gardiner Means as long ago as 1932, in *The Modern Corporation and Private Property.* They contended that stock ownership had been widely dispersed and that corporate management had been separated from stock ownership and from stock owners and now operated independently of the profit motive.

Although it is granted by practically all that corporate power is still very great, current theory suggests that it is self-restrained and socially responsible, a power in equilibrium with the state and the labor union. For many, it is an article of faith that its potential for social harm will not and could not be exercised.

There is a notion that corporate power is held in trust for the community. The corporate leadership, writes David Riesman in *The Lonely Crowd,* is "coming more and more to think of themselves as trustees for their beneficiaries [252]." The corporation, writes Berle, "has been compelled to assume in appreciable part the role of conscience-carrier of twentieth-century American society." Further, he says, "the corporation is now, essentially, a nonstatist political institution, and its directors are in the same boat with public officeholders."[1]

Such assertions assume that the power of the stockholder is no longer a factor of major significance. They further assume that the corporate leadership has no interests that are in conflict with the "public's"—and that it shares none with the amorphous and presumably constantly expanding ranks of stockholders. In this view, the operating executives— the men who make the short- and intermediate-range decisions for the large corporations—have displaced the directors

[1] *The 20th Century Capitalist Revolution,* New York, 1954, 182.

as architects of fundamental, long-range policies. . . . And so, it is suggested, the corporate managers, freed from responsibility to those whose only incentive is profit, have brought new motives to business leadership.

But the real question, the heart of the matter, is whether there is in fact a small group of persons in a position to exercise control over the corporate structure. If there is such a group, the matter of whether they actually utilize this power is secondary—the overriding consideration is, Do they have such power? It doesn't matter how they exercise this power, whether for their particular interests or for those of society as a whole. The philosophy of their views may be debatable; the anatomy of their power is not.

The facts, in brief, are these: In 1955 the 200 top nonfinancial companies—most of which dominated their respective industries as price and policy leaders—directly owned 43.0 percent of the total assets of 435,000 nonfinancial corporations; this amounted to at least 18.3 percent of the total national reproducible tangible assets of $891 billion.

These corporations were controlled by approximately 2,500 men—and probably even fewer.

These men, in both direct ownership of economic assets and control over the corporate structure, are the most important single group in the American economic elite.

INTERLOCKING DIRECTORATES

Interlocking directorates, whereby a director of one corporation also sits on the board of one or more other corporations, are a key device for concentrating corporate power, since they enable one corporation to wield influence over one or more others. The director representing Company A can, by sitting on the board of Company B, exert influence over it to increase its financial cooperation with Company A or make purchases from it. He can also act to prevent Company B from manufacturing a competing product or diversifying into a field occupied by Company A.

The Temporary National Economic Committee discovered that in 1939, within the top 200 corporations, there were 3,511 directorships held by about 2,500 persons. Offhand, this would seem to suggest that interlocking directorships were not very significant.

But let us look at corporations that rank below the top 200 in size. It is, after all, much more likely that a giant corporation would attempt to influence a corporation smaller than itself than one larger or the same size. When one tabulates the number of directorships in corporations of every size held by the directors of the top 200 corporations, a pattern of extensive interlocking directorships emerges, involving a very large percentage of the top directors. Here, then, is the dominant fact of economic control: the top 200 corporations cooperate with each other and exert influence within innumerable smaller companies. Generally, of course, the larger corporation sends its representative to the board of the smaller firm.

In 1957, Sidney J. Weinberg, of the investment house of Goldman, Sachs, sat on not only five boards among the top 200 corporations, but six boards of smaller companies; T. W. Collins, an officer-director of Crown-Zellerbach, was on seven boards below the top 200; and James Bruce, a director of National Dairy, sat on three boards among the top 200 and 13 lesser ones.

Interlocking directorates are classified by the Federal Trade Commission into seven major forms:

1. Between competing firms—whether direct (one company's director sits on another company's board) or indirect (two companies share a director whose primary tie is with a third company)—and thereby control or eliminate competition. In 1946, five of the 12 big meat packers were indirectly interlocked, 16 of the 23 largest sugar companies were directly and indirectly interlocked, and 17 of the 20 largest petroleum companies were interlocked.

2. Between companies in related industries that are interested in preventing diversification into directly competitive products. Such interlocking exists in the glass industry, for example, so that

bottle and sheet-glass makers will not encroach on each other.

3. Between companies in a single industry that face similar problems and share a community of interests, whether direct or indirect. Thus, the four largest electrical-machinery corporations were indirectly interlocked in 1946.

4. Between purchasing company and supplier, whose relationship generally involves a strategic advantage to the purchasing company. The food industry is heavily interlocked with the container industry, the automobile companies with the parts manufacturers. This is the most important form of interlocking.

5. Between producer and distributor, for the purpose of gaining preferential markets. Thus Westinghouse Air Brake Company is linked with most of the major manufacturers of railroad cars and locomotives, and the glass-making companies with the distilleries and drug companies.

6. Between corporation and financial institution, to provide adequate credit for the corporation and possible denial of credit to competitors. Myriad examples of this exist.

7. Between companies with common ownership. The General Motors–Du Pont –U.S. Rubber–Ethyl group is an excellent case in point.

The annual proxy statement rarely gives details of a company's contacts and transactions with the firms with which it has common directors. Among the proxy statements of the 100 top industrialists for 1957, I was able to find only one significant policy statement on intercorporate relations. Republic Steel, in a statement that innumerable other corporations could have made just as well, frankly declared, "In accordance with the policy of the Corporation Messrs. White, Patton, Foy, and Hancock, as well as other officers of the Corporation, serve as officers and directors of certain companies in which the Corporation has a substantial (but not controlling) stock interest, from which it purchases raw materials and/or to which it has advanced funds for construction or exploration programs." The directors and major officers of Republic Steel each sit on an average of six other boards. No corporation in a position of dependency on one of the top 200 corporations can refuse the giant a seat on its board, and thus a potent voice in the guidance of its affairs, without risking the loss of an important, if not decisive, segment of its sales.

THE DIRECTORS

Now let us undertake to discover if the corporate director is, in fact, the passive yet statesmanlike creature that is portrayed by modern theories. To accomplish this, we shall examine in some detail the nature of power and control in the 100 largest industrial corporations, as ranked by assets, in 1957. (Of these, 72 were also in the top 100 in 1937.) These 100 corporations accounted for 54 percent of the assets of the 200 largest nonfinancial corporations in 1957—compared to only 37 percent in 1937—or about one-quarter of all nonfinancial corporation assets and one-tenth of total national assets. The form and extent of control within these 100 corporations is significant, both in measuring the concentration of wealth within the very small elite and in evaluating the dominant theories on the nature of corporate power in America.

In the largest industrial corporations, the directors are neither a passive group nor at odds with the basic policies and interests of management. The reason is simple: Most company directors are also members of management. The trend in this direction has been decisive. In 1937–39, 36 percent of the directors of the top industrials were also key officers in their respective companies. By 1957, that figure was 50 percent. This meant, taking into account interlocking directorates, that the majority of the 1,477 directors of the 100 top companies were active officers in some of those companies. In 47 of the top 100, officer-directors held absolute majorities. So with most directors, it is obvious how they exert power: They are actively engaged in the management of the largest corporations.

A National Industrial Conference Board study of directors of 638 manufacturing corporations of varied sizes in

1959, found that 46 percent were officers as well as directors of their companies. Another 17 percent were "substantial stockholders" who were not officers, and 10 percent represented interested financial institutions.

There remains the problem of how power is exercised by directors who are not also officers.

Some directors, as we have seen in our discussion of interlocking directorates, exert influence because they represent other, and usually larger, corporations. Backed by their primary company, they are in a position to demand conformity to certain policies. Whether or not they exert this power is immaterial. The fact is that they can.

For a director of one firm, obtaining a connection as director in other firms— and preferably a large number of them —is motivated by the realization that this power in reserve may be useful to his primary firm or himself. General Motors, for example, was helped in monopolizing the bus-manufacturing industry by the fact that a number of bankers sat on transit-company boards of directors. Eager for GM accounts, these bankers intervened with transit managers on behalf of GM buses.

In 1939, the top officers and directors of each of the 97 largest manufacturing corporations collectively owned an average of 7.0 percent of the *total* number of shares in their own company. This is a conservative estimate based on far more abundant data than are available for the present period.

Now let us investigate the stock ownership of directors. From the annual proxy statements and documents filed with the Securities and Exchange Commission, we can arrive at a *minimum* percentage for the ownership of *voting* stock by the directors of the 100 largest industrial corporations. In 1957, the board of directors of these corporations owned or represented an average of 9.9 percent of its shares. That figure would probably be increased by several percentage points if it were possible to include the stock ownership in several closely owned giants that do not issue proxy statements. In only 23 of these 100 companies are

directors listed as owning more than 10 percent of the voting stock; in 36, they are listed as owning less than 1 percent. As in 1937, the vast majority of stock owned by directors is held by no more than 300 men.

The matter of stock ownership by directors only begins with the figure of 10 percent. We know that large holdings are synonymous with power; however, their absence does not necessarily rule out the presence of power in some subtler or more complex form. It is much more likely that we are ignorant of crucial information. It is important to press the matter further, to persevere in the search for the location of such power by assuming that it is not necessarily diffused.

Let us first look back a generation, and examine the 1937–39 directorates of the 72 of 1957's 100 top industrials for which we have information. It is quite clear that many of the important stockholding groups of the late 1930's are still in the same controlling positions. In board after board, the same family names appear in 1957 and in 1937–39—even when these people are no longer listed as having significant stock holdings. It is especially intriguing to find that the family pattern is very noticeable in 22 of the 72 corporations, and that in 1957, these 22 had an average stock ownership by directors of only 3.1 percent, which very substantially pulled down the overall average.

The splitting of blocks of stocks among family members for tax purposes, or the placing of the stocks in professionally managed trusts and investment companies, where identities can be obscured, may have practical value for the corporate elite. But these moves can hardly be regarded as significant changes in stock ownership.

In 1937–39 the Phipps family, via Bessemer Securities Corporation, owned 9.7 percent of the stock of International Paper. In 1957, Ogden Phipps, chairman of Bessemer, sat on the International Paper board and was listed as owning 0.1 percent of its stock. The Mellon family owned more than 50 percent of Gulf Oil in 1937–39, but the two Mellons who sat on Gulf's board in 1957 were listed as owning a mere 6.5 percent. The Mathers owned 9.3 percent of Youngstown Sheet and Tube in 1937–39, but were listed, through their one director, as owning only 0.5 percent in 1957.

The Du Ponts owned 15 percent of U.S. Rubber in 1937–39, but in 1957, their representative, G. P. Edwards, who sat on the board was listed as owning virtually nothing. The Jones, Laughlin, and Robinson families owned about one-third of the Jones & Laughlin stock in 1937–39, but in 1957, their three board seats derived from their combined ownership of 0.5 percent. The McCormick family owned about one-third of International Harvester in 1937–39, but the two family members on the board in 1957 owned a mere 1.2 percent. The Levis family owned 16.8 percent of Owens-Illinois Glass in 1937–39; they had two board members but less than 1.5 percent of the stock in 1957. The Root family held 3.6 percent of this company's stock in 1937–39, but in 1957, its one director was listed for about 0.3 percent.

In search of some definition of the top elite, Robert A. Gordon, in *Business Leadership in the Large Corporation* (1945), took the 20 largest shareholders —including banks, trusts, foundations, insurance, and other corporations, as well as individuals—of each of the 200 largest corporations in 1937–39 (as determined by the TNEC), which he pruned to 176 by eliminating subsidiaries. He found that the cumulative top 20 stockholders owned an average of 28.6 percent of the market value of common stock. In 101 out of 183 stock issues, they owned at least 20 percent, or what is for all practical purposes a controlling share. Individuals or their legal devices, such as trusts and personal holding companies, owned half of the stock held by this tiny group of no more than 4,000 shareholders. In effect, they were the dominant shareowner influence in corporate affairs.

Here the concentration of stock ownership in a small group is plainly seen. But what it means in terms of economic power is less clear. It is debatable how much this group can do toward obtaining control, if they do not already have

it, over the corporations they own. However, the large increase in the number of corporate proxy fights in recent years and the success of insurgents in about one-third of these indicate that the power of key stockholders is no myth.

In many corporations whose stock is highly concentrated in a very small group, key stockholders choose not to exert power through direct representation on the board of directors and in top officer groups. Obviously their major concern as stockholders is profits and investment security, which, as indicated by the consistently high net corporate income and the restricted distribution of dividends to lower personal taxes, has been well served by the existing officers and directors. Since no major American corporation has ever sought to pursue a policy of enlightened public activities at the cost of basic profit margins, stockholders have never been forced to exert power for this reason.

The power of both stockholders and managers, however, exists within a small elite whose relation to society is rarely changed by disputes within its own ranks. In 1937–39, there was no visible center of control through ownership in only 58 of the top 176 corporations. In 83 corporations, ultimate power rested with family stockholding groups, some owning as little as 4 percent and actively involved in management, most owning much more and inactive. Thirty-five companies were dominated by corporate groups who were in turn owned by large shareholders.

Because of the continued, if not intensified, concentration of shares in a very small proportion of the stockholders, it must be concluded that the most powerful corporate giants still remain within the control of a small group of men. This was at least as true in 1957 as in the late 1930's, since the means of control have become more centralized in the intervening years.

MANAGEMENT

Berle and Means have alleged that the top officers of the giant corporations no longer own any significant percentage of the stock and that, as professional managers, they do not have the same interests as the stockholders. The new managers, it is claimed, are oriented toward rationalizing and consolidating the position of the corporation, are more sensitive to public opinion, and are concerned with avoiding risk ventures that might maximize profits but would endanger the basic security of the corporation.

Whether the "great faceless corporations [are] 'owned' by no one and run by self-designated 'managers'" can be settled by the answers to two crucial questions that have been ignored by the theorists: (1) How much stock do the key managers own in the top corporations they run? (2) How much stock does management, as a class, own in all corporations, and thus to what extent do they share the profit motive of stockholders? Is it true, as corporation lawyer David T. Bazelon put it, that the manager of the giant corporation is "not a capitalist at all; he is a new fish"?[2]

The issue here is not the concentration of economic power but the motivation of managerial actions by tangible incentives. However small their percentage of the stock may be, it is exceedingly important to their personal fortunes and, therefore, a crucial motivating factor in their corporate role. In early 1957, 25 General Motors officers owned an average of 11,500 shares each. Collectively, their holdings would have been inconsequential if they had chosen to try to obtain control of GM through their stocks. Yet each of these men had a personal stake of roughly a half million dollars in the company—plus the tantalizing prospect that over the next decade or two the corporation's growth and profits might double or treble the value of his stock and make him an exceptionally wealthy man.

The corporate executive is tied to the profit performance of the corporate system in many tangible ways. But the discussions by Berle, Riesman, and others of the separation of management from the profit incentive, and from stock in particular, is based on a failure to appre-

ciate the nature of the executive compensation system. Most serious of all, they have ignored the major, and potentially revolutionary, impact of the stock option on the corporate executive.

The stock option, originated in 1950, has committed top management more strongly than ever before to the corporation's profit position, because without profits, the options are largely worthless. By 1957, option plans had been instituted by 77 percent of the manufacturing corporations listed on the New York or American Stock Exchanges. Of the 100 largest industrials, only 13 did not have option plans in 1959, and in most of these corporations, there was heavy stock ownership by directors. Of the 87 with option plans, the 83 for which public data was available had granted key officers options on an average of 1.9 percent of their outstanding voting stock by 1959.

Suggestive of future trends is the percentage of outstanding stock reserved for executive options. By 1960, Inland Steel had assigned the equivalent of 11 percent of its outstanding voting stock for options. Ford, in 1960, reserved 6.7 percent of its outstanding shares for future options. If this trend continues, it will further strengthen the tie between management and stock, especially in companies whose management holdings are now comparatively small.

Top corporation executives are very well-paid men. In 1958, the median income for the highest-paid 1,700 was $73,600. But Berle and the others assume that they, unlike most others in this income class, will not buy stock. The fact is that the corporate executive *does* buy stock. Thus his personal fortunes are bound not only to the money-making success of his own company but also to that of the larger corporate structure in which he has invested. Theoretically, it would not make a great deal of difference if the managers had, in fact, no personal interest in the dividend performance or market value of stocks, since it has never been shown how the managers differ, in practice and theory, from the stockholding elite.

In fact, the managerial class **is the**

[2] "Facts and Fictions of U.S. Capitalism," *The Reporter*, September 17, 1959, 43, 45.

largest single group in the stockholding population, and a greater proportion of this class owns stock than any other. The statistics: 44.8 percent of all administrative officials—top company officials and managers in corporations, banks, and the like—own stock. For operating supervisory officials—managers of medium-size and small companies, department heads of these companies or larger organizations, and kindred types—the figure was 19.4 percent. These are the results of the Brookings Institution's 1952 census of stockholders, which also showed that 6.3 percent of all shareholders were administrative executives and 13.1 percent were operating supervisory officials.

How much stock does the managerial class own? We know that spending units owning $100,000 or more in marketable stock in 1949 accounted for at least 65 to 71 percent of the total individual ownership, and we can reasonably assume that this figure is valid after 1949, since stock concentration has been fairly stable. Of all the spending units in that category in 1957, nearly half—47.4 percent, to be precise—were from the managerial class. Also, one-fifth of the managerial spending units owning stock in 1957 possessed more than $100,000 worth.

It is impossible to give a precise figure on the percentage of stock owned by the managerial class, but these figures indicate that the managers own a very large proportion, if not well over the majority, of shares in the United States.

Management, then, is the class most interested in the highest dividends, in both their own firms and others. And taking into account the greater prevalence of stock ownership among top management shown by the Brookings study, as well as the high incomes and stock options in this group, it becomes clear that the interest of top executives in stock is undoubtedly the most important among those in the managerial class.

To talk of a separation between management and major stockholders in the United States is obviously quite impossible; they are virtually one and the same.

The concentration of economic power in a very small elite is an indisputable fact. This power is a function of both their direct ownership in the corporate structure and their ability to control it. Their possession of savings and wealth is possible because of the continuing basic inequality of income that is simply a part of a larger pattern of inequality in the United States.

The implications of this intense centralization of economic power are twofold. First, the concentration of income allocates a large share of the consumption of goods to a small proportion of the population. For a public policy directed toward maintenance of full employment through full consumption, this fact raises major obstacles for working within the existing income distribution structure. Second, and more important for this study, a social theory assuming a democratized economic system—or even a trend in this direction—is quite obviously not in accord with social reality. Whether the men who control industry are socially responsive or trustees of the social welfare is quite another matter; it is one thing to speculate about their motivations, another to generalize about economic facts. And even if we assume that these men act benevolently toward their workers and the larger community, their actions still would not be the result of social control through a formal democratic structure and group participation, which are the essentials for democracy; they would be an arbitrary *noblesse oblige* by the economic elite. When discussing the existing corporate system, it would be more realistic to drop all references to democracy.

The real questions are: (1) Do a small group of very wealthy men have the power to guide industry, and thereby much of the total economy, toward ends that they decide upon as compatible with their own interests? (2) Do they own and control the major corporations?

The answers must inevitably be affirmative.

Adolf A. Berle, Jr.

THE FISSION OF PROPERTY

Adolf A. Berle, Jr. first attracted wide public attention in 1932, when he and Gardiner Means published *The Modern Corporation and Private Property*. In *The 20th Century Capitalist Revolution*, Berle explored the self-imposed restraints of business leaders in the use of their power. In this passage from his book *Power Without Property*, he discusses the changing relationship between property ownership and control in the past, and then turns to the rise of fiduciary institutions, a new force in the American economy.

PROPERTY is in essence relationship between an individual (or perhaps a group of individuals) and a tangible or intangible thing. (The Roman Law called it a "*Res*"; the common law still does.) We have to interpret the word "thing" rather broadly. There are incorporeal as well as physical "things." Bodies of knowledge, written and unwritten, in the technical laboratories of many corporations have little physical substance, but they are so real that they can be bought and sold. Their money-worth often exceeds the worth of many items in a corporation's plant and property account, despite the accounting tradition that "conservatism" requires "patents and processes" to be carried at nominal valuation. In speaking of property, we here include incorporeal as well as corporeal items.

Both in fact and in law, the norm of property is thought to be some "thing" capable of being possessed, that is, reduced to or kept in control of an individual or individuals—the "proprietor" or in English, the "owner." In law, the essence of proprietorship was the owner's capacity to exclude everyone but himself from possession, use, or control—subject to certain overriding rights of the sovereign State. Our great-grandfathers not only owned but possessed their farms, forges, grist mills, and modest enterprises. The typical conception of private property was that of things in possession of one or more individuals. Current semantics conjures up this picture even now.

Growth of the corporate system changed that. Change was gradual and somewhat insidious. Two or three individuals "incorporated" their business; it was still small, still capable of being possessed. They were stockholders but they were also directors and managers. Legal title now inhered in the corporation; the stockholders had beneficial ownership in the corporate property and as managers had actual possession of it. So long as the business and the corporation continued small, the stockholders largely determined what the corporate title holder actually did. The fact that the unit of property had been marked for later split-up was not apparent. Enlargement of the corporation made it evident that fissures on the surface of the property represented a clear division.

The legal entity known as the corporation now emerges as an owner of the property. Any relation it had to things was necessarily carried on by individuals. The individuals became the board of directors and the officers and employees of the corporation, not its stockholders. Possession, originally the hallmark of a proprietor, now devolved on managers—at least, as long as the property was small enough so that it could be "possessed" at all.

As early as the end of the nineteenth century, many corporations had title to

Abridged from *Power Without Property, A New Development In American Political Economy*, © 1959 by A. A. Berle, Jr., 60–64, 69–76. Reprinted by permission of Harcourt, Brace, and World, Inc., and of Sidgwick & Jackson, Ltd.

so many "things" that not even management could "possess" them. Top management perhaps actually "possessed" their offices and furnishings. Sub-managers, district superintendents, plant administrators, and so forth held the actual possession of the bulk of the things with which the corporation dealt—subject, it is true, to the direction of the management. But suddenly we find ourselves using different language.

Capacity to give an order in respect of property is one thing; the fact of having it in your possession is rather different. "Possession" has somehow become diluted. Under the corporate system it is no longer (assuming it still exists) the relation of man to thing; it is the relation of a man to another man, another man whose subordinate has actual control of the thing. We have begun, in a word, to encounter the vocabulary of power while thinking in terms of a property frame. The fact has diverged from the fiction.

The story that a new president of General Electric was once thrown out of the corporation's main plant at Schenectady by a night watchman who did not know him is undoubtedly apocryphal, but sufficiently illustrates the divergence. The actual possessor of the plant on that night in that case was the night watchman. The president was merely an individual who had power to give orders to the night watchman if he could make them good. He was agent of an impersonal corporation which in law was the "owner." But a corporation is at worst a legal fiction, and at strongest an impersonal entity resting on a congeries of habitual and continuing personal relationships without itself having personality.

Meanwhile we have lost our former proprietor and must go back to find him.

When our original unit of property first entered the corporate system, he held stock—pieces of paper. They conveyed to him several extremely valuable privileges. Among other things he could receive dividends as and when the corporation—that is to say, its board of directors—declared and paid them. He could receive a share of the corporate property if it decided to go out of business, reduce its property to distributable form, and liquidate. These gave him a right to receive a fraction of current profits, and a potential share in assets in the improbable case that the corporation while still solvent determined to wind up its affairs.

His third right, valuable in certain circumstances, was the right to vote. If he held or could mobilize around him a majority of the votes inherent in shares, he could name the board of directors. He could refuse to re-elect them at the end of their stated term. This was the substitute for his former personal power to possess, to exclude others from, and to control the things which have now passed to the corporation as title holder. This capacity gave him no right whatever to a physical relationship with the things forming the corporation's assets. Ownership of a share of stock in the American Telephone & Telegraph Company gives the holder no right whatever to go off with a telephone pole.

Twentieth-century dispersion of stock and its voting rights among many thousands or hundreds of thousands of stockholders in practice commonly reduced its voting power almost to ceremonial status. But there always was possibility that a stockholder or group of stockholders or some insurgent committee could mobilize enough stockholders, aggregate enough of these vestigial rights, and emerge with power to upset management. This amounted to little more than the right to execute a very rare revolution. The widely publicized proxy fights and battles for control of management which enliven the financial pages are actually the rarest exception in corporate life. Even those, as a rule, commonly concern the small corporations. Not once in a decade is the control of a minor giant thus threatened. Managements of the major giants are, for practical purposes, impregnable.

Now this stock certificate, carrying a right to receive certain distributions and to vote, begins to split. Once it is bought by a fiduciary institution, be it pension trust, mutual fund, or insurance company, that institution becomes the "stockholder," holds legal title to the stock certificate and to its right to vote. But it has by contract dedicated the dividends or other benefits to distribution among beneficiaries under the pension contract, the fund arrangement, or the insurance policy. The one remaining power by which the recipient of corporate profits might have direct relation to corporate ownership has been divided from the benefit itself.

Actually, the division has gone deeper than that. The fiduciary recipient of dividends from a corporation no longer has relation of any kind even to the stock certificate, let alone to the corporate management; of course, far less to the real property. The beneficiary of a life insurance policy or pension trust under settled law has no interest in the stock certificates held by his pension trustees or by his life insurance company. He has only a contract (perhaps in substance a status) relationship to the pension trust or the insurance company. Even in the tenuous reasoning of the law he has ceased to have discernible relationship to the things with which the corporation works.

*   *   *

Our former owner-possessor has likewise changed position. In some ways he is harder to follow because less visible; but we can trace the main lines of his evolution. . . .

In his first stage he began by ceding his direct legal relationship to the *Res* when he turned it over to the corporation and took instead a piece of paper called a "stock certificate." But he, perhaps with his family, retained absolute stockholder control. We noted that his stock certificates represented a right to receive dividends when his board of directors declared them and a share in assets if the corporation should be liquidated (this rarely occurs in the case of any great corporation). The stock certificates also included the right to vote—which if one had more than a majority in practice meant the right to nominate and to express a choice for or against the men who are to be directors. In fact, though not in technical law, it meant power to

give them orders. The voting right might or might not have any real relation to the proportion of assets he (or, in strict accuracy, his grandfather or distant predecessor in title) contributed as capital to the organization about 1918. For one thing, the handling of voting rights when a corporation is set up is itself a fine art. Sufficient illustration is the fact that under most corporation laws a Class A stock, roughly representing a contribution of $100 per share, may be allotted one vote per share, while a Class B stock, each share representing, say, a contribution of $1.00, may also have one vote. In that case (there are many of them) the Class B holder has 100 times the voting right of Class A per dollar invested. This original arrangement, set out in the certificate of incorporation, sets the stage for future development. As long as our original owner had in his own possession enough shares of stock to dominate the annual meeting, because he had a majority of votes, or so long as with three or four friends, he could accumulate a majority, he had what the financial districts call "control." Control is, quite simply, capacity to make or unmake a board of directors.

Control is a great deal, but by no means everything. Directors when he had elected them were not, and in law are not now, his "agents." They are at liberty to defy his instructions. Their judgment, not his, must govern until he replaces them. Discharge of directors appears simpler than it actually is. Stockholders who discharge directors save for weighty and adequate cause are apt to find it difficult to secure the services of other able men in their place. The banks with which the corporation deals grow nervous; banks are easily upset. As in the case of a President who wishes to throw out a Cabinet Member without damaging himself, the reasons must be cogent and the record well documented. The management responsibility, for the moment, is thrown back on controlling stockholders who may or may not have or be able to attract the requisite combination of energy, character, and talent to deal with the situation. In violent changes of management, the enterprise is apt to suffer.

Stockholder "control" in a large enterprise does not ordinarily continue for any long space of time. Normally, a generation is its span. The really great enterprises now are commonly not "stockholder controlled," though there are a few striking exceptions. The Ford Motor Company is still dominated by the Ford family, which thoughtfully retained the voting control, though it donated the bulk of Ford shares to the Ford Foundation. The DuPont de Nemours Company is still controlled by the DuPont family, through a series of devices including among others a family corporation, Christiania Securities Company. The Mellon family probably dominates Aluminum Corporation of America. In trade, the Hartford family still controls the Great Atlantic & Pacific Tea Company— a giant in its field. But these situations are exceptions among the couple of hundred authentic behemoths in American business. In any event multiplication of family offspring, time, and the ineluctable solvent power of inheritance taxes may be counted on to compel eventual dispersion.

The second stage below absolute stockholder control is called in financial markets "working control." It exists where an individual or group has less than a majority of the stock, but has sufficient affinity with or influence over the board of directors of the corporation so that existing directors will use their power to name a management slate to send out proxies to the stockholders along lines suggested by the holders of "working control." But again we have introduced an essentially political element. The focus of communication between corporation and stockholder is the corporate management, acting through its president or secretary who acts at the direction of the board of directors. A substantial percentage of stockholders with small holdings practically always can be counted on to follow the lead of the management through sheer inertia. In practice this means that they will sign and return any proxy sent them by the management. Another proportion of stockholders can be counted on to do nothing. If the votes of the group that invariably

follows management are added to those of the large (though nonmajority) stockholder, the result is "working control." To maintain "working control" in this situation, the large stockholder must therefore have and hold close relationship with the management. The size of holdings needed to maintain "working control" varies inversely with the breadth of distribution, that is, the greater the number of small stockholdings of the stock of the company in question, the less stock is needed to maintain (in alliance with management) "working control."

At this stage, the "owner," if a stockholder or stockholding group can be thus described, must maintain a variety of political relationship with the management. The power is shared. The management position is quite possibly as strong as the stockholding position. Should the holder of "working control" decide to canvass his fellow stockholders for the purpose of overturning the management, the result may well be in doubt. Most of the famed "proxy contests" or struggles for control occur when a holder has or has accumulated large holdings of voting stock through less than a majority, but does not have that relationship with management which enables him through them to secure the votes of the small stockholders who habitually and blindly follow management lead. His precise purpose is to put in a management with which he will have such a relationship.

This second stage probably was the typical situation in American industry from about 1914 to 1928, though figures have never been compiled. It still exists as a major factor in a good many large corporations. Though it is continually diminishing, "working control" is a presently familiar location of industrial power.

Parenthetically, we may mark a parallel change in the social structure of the United States. At the turn of the century "absolute control"—the stockholder or group who had ceased to possess the property but could dominate any management—was probably the norm. This required concentration of stockholdings in the vaults of individuals of great wealth. It was part of the plutocratic age which prevailed through the last three decades of the nineteenth and the first decade of the twentieth century, leaving a reminiscent mark on the culture of the United States. The palace communities like Newport, Lenox, and the Massachusetts North Shore were creations of that era; it inspired literature like Edith Wharton's *The Age of Innocence*, and is well described in the early chapters of Margaret Coit's recent biography of Bernard Baruch. Henry Adams wrote of this period that in it all judgments in America were ultimately made by wealth. The picture of America as a plutocracy has survived overseas decades after the fact has passed into history. Perhaps there is a passing recrudescence of the era in Texas, due chiefly to certain accepted loopholes in income tax law, to fortunate oil discoveries, and to a mass upsurge in need for petroleum.

The decade of great expansion, the years of the First World War, and the fantastic, expansive, and catastrophic speculative years which continued until 1929 ended the existence of absolute stockholder control as a norm. It was succeeded by the "working control" stage; but by then many of the great corporations had already passed into the third phase—"management control."

"Management control" is a phrase meaning merely that no large concentrated stockholding exists which maintains a close working relationship with the management or is capable of challenging it, so that the board of directors may regularly expect a majority, composed of small and scattered holdings, to follow their lead. Thus they need not consult with anyone when making up their slates of directors, and may simply request their stockholders to sign and send in a ceremonial proxy. They select their own successors. Theoretically it is possible for someone outside management to mobilize the army of small stockholders, aggregate their votes, and displace the existing directors. But the task is huge, the expense great, and the results problematic. It has happened so rarely that the possibility may be discarded.

This is the locus of power over and the norm of control of the bulk of American industry now. Nominal power still resides in the stockholders; actual power in the board of directors. The New York Stock Exchange has calculated that there are in the United States between six and seven million holders of stock (the figure is at best an estimate). Included in this figure are a relatively small number who hold large blocks. Probably the 50,000 largest holders of stocks could still exercise a powerful force if they worked together—which they do not and probably cannot. Included in this top stratum are surviving individual holders of "working control" of which (as noted) there remain a good many; most of this second-stage group are also apparently outward bound for elimination.

Essentially these stockholders, though still politely called "owners," are passive. They have the right to receive only. The condition of their being is that they do not interfere in management. Neither in law nor, as a rule, in fact do they have that capacity. This is why . . . we designate them "passive-receptive"; any ability in them to create, or even to labor upon the *Res*, has gone out of the picture. A stockholder may, to be sure, take a job with his company. But his relation to the *Res* has become that of jobholder, not of owner. Any possibility of initiative on his part has passed. The case of the grandson of a former owner, though himself wealthy and holding a financially valuable block of stock, who must nevertheless (if he wishes a career) seek employment like everyone else, qualifying by his ability rather than by his stockholder's vote, is familiar in American business. As a creator or initiator he has been quietly displaced, just as the owner of a farm who sells it and takes a job with an adjacent factory has been displaced. His relative poverty or relative wealth has little to do with his career opportunity. These are the six or seven million "owners"—stockholders—of American industry. It had to be that way. Operating a large-unit productive system like that of present day America necessarily concentrates decision-making power while the corporate system distributes wealth.

Now appears the fourth stage. In this situation emerge the newer mechanisms, the fiduciary institutions, by which these dispersed stockholdings are once more becoming concentrated. True, the number of individuals expecting to receive benefits from the stock through the medium of these institutions is vastly increasing. But as distribution of income increases, voting power becomes increasingly concentrated.

So we discern the latest and apparently inescapable future norm in our chassé of property and power. Economic benefits by way of dividend or other distributions accruing to shares of stock are received by these impersonal institutions to be redistributed to their policyholders or to their pension beneficiaries—but wholly without direct relationship between the recipients and the stock, let alone the corporation. A pensionnaire or policyholder may conceivably have in the shadowy beyond (especially in a mutual company or cooperative) some astronomically distant and purely theoretical possibility of sharing in the assets of the insurance company or trust. But for all practical purposes he has a contract right to a stated sum of money only. His pension trust or his insurance company may have working, or even absolute, control of the Union Pacific Railroad or the United States Steel Corporation—but he has no part whatever in that. His right is to receive the face value of his insurance policy when he reaches age 65 or dies, or an annuity, or something of the sort. Or his right is to

receive a pension amounting to, say, 50 percent of his average pay for the five years preceding retirement provided he has been an employee of the corporation or possibly of the industry for a stated period of years. Put differently, his right is to receive money only, and it depends on a status position of some kind based on his having fulfilled a stated set of conditions. He would not know—and it would be immaterial if he did know—what voting power his insurance company or his pension trust held with respect to the management of Union Pacific or United States Steel. He could not influence the situation in any case. He is, if possible, more passive-receptive than ever. His relation to the "things" that make up American industry has simply ceased.

So, as noted, divorce between men and industrial things is becoming complete. A Communist revolution could not accomplish that more completely. Certainly it could not do so with the same finesse. When a Russian Communist government says to the workers that "the people" own the instruments of production but it will take care of them, it is assigning to its population a passive-receptive position closely comparable to the one we are studying. The difference lies in the fact that the criteria for reception are different, and that the political State exercises the power factor now gradually but steadily being aggregated under the American system in nonpolitical but equally impersonal fiduciary institutions.

John K. Galbraith

THE TECHNOSTRUCTURE

Few present-day scholars have done more than Harvard economist John K. Galbraith to enlighten the masses in economics. In this selection from *The New Industrial State,* he historically traces the correlation between power and the control or possession of land, labor, and capital. Concluding that group expertise currently overshadows the authority of the individual in American business enterprise, Galbraith suggests that power has passed to a new factor of production.

POWER goes to the factor which is hardest to obtain or hardest to replace. In precise language it adheres to the one that has the greatest inelasticity of supply at the margin. This inelasticity may be the result of a natural shortage, or an effective control over supply by some human agency, or both.

In its age, if one had land then labor and capital (in the meager amounts required) could be readily obtained. But to have labor and operating capital did not so readily insure that a man could get land. There was an admixture, here, of cause and effect. Because land provided special access to economic and larger power, steps were taken, as through the laws of entail, to confine possession to the privileged or noble caste. And this, in turn, limited the opportunities for acquiring it and further increased the economic power and social authority which, from one generation to the next, land conferred on its owner.

In the age of capital, land was readily available in the minor amounts required for industrial enterprise and increasingly so for agriculture. Labor continued to be plentiful. Now possession of land and labor did not allow one to command capital; but with capital, land and labor could easily be obtained. Capital now accorded power in the enterprise and in consequence in the society.

Should it happen that capital were to become abundant, or redundant, and thus be readily increased or replaced, the power it confers, both in the enterprise and in the society, would be expected to suffer. This would seem especially probable if, at the same time, some other factor of production should prove increasingly difficult to add or replace.

. . . In the industrial system, while capital is used in large amounts, it is, at least in peacetime, even more abundantly supplied. The tendency to an excess of savings, and the need for an offsetting strategy by the state, is an established and well-recognized feature of the Keynesian economy. And savings, we have seen, are supplied by the industrial enterprise to itself as part of its planning. There is high certainty as to their availability, for this is the purpose of the planning.

At the same time the requirements of technology and planning have greatly increased the need of the industrial enterprise for specialized talent and for its organization. The industrial system must rely, in the main, on external sources for this talent. Unlike capital it is not something that the firm can supply to itself. To be effective this talent must also be brought into effective association with itself. It must be in an organization. Given a competent business organization, capital is now ordinarily available. But the mere possession of capital is now no guarantee that the requisite talent can be obtained and organized. One should expect, from past experience, to find a new shift of power in the industrial enterprise, this one from capital to organized intelligence. And one would expect that this shift would be reflected in the deployment of power in the society at large.

This has, indeed, occurred. It is a shift of power as between the factors of production which matches that which occurred from land to capital in the advanced countries beginning two centuries ago. It is an occurrence of the last fifty years and is still going on. A dozen matters of commonplace observation—the loss of power by stockholders in the modern corporation, the impregnable position of the successful corporate management, the dwindling social magnetism of the banker, the air of quaintness that attaches to the suggestion that the United States is run from Wall Street, the increasingly energetic search for industrial talent, the new prestige of education and educators—all attest the point.

This shift of power has been disguised because, as was once true of land, the position of capital is imagined to be immutable. That power should be elsewhere seems unnatural and those who so argue seem to be in search of frivolous novelty. And it has been disguised because power has not gone to another of the established factors as they are celebrated in conventional economic pedagogy. It has not passed to labor. Labor has won limited authority over its pay and working conditions but none over the enterprise. And it still tends to abundance. If overly abundant savings are not used, the first effect is unemployment; if savings are used one consequence is a substitution of machine processes for unskilled labor and standard skills. Thus unskilled labor and workers with conventional skills suffer, along with the capitalist, from an abundance of capital.

Nor has power passed to the classical entrepreneur—the individual who once used his access to capital to bring it into combination with the other factors of production. He is a diminishing figure in the industrial system. Apart from access to capital, his principal qualifications were imagination, capacity for decision and courage in risking money including, not infrequently, his own. None of these qualifications are especially important for organizing intelligence or effective in competing with it.

Power has, in fact, passed to what anyone in search of novelty might be justified in calling a new factor of production. This is the association of men of diverse technical knowledge, experience or other talent which modern industrial technology and planning require. It extends from the leadership of the modern industrial enterprise down to just short of the labor force and embraces a large number of people and a large variety of talent. It is on the effectiveness of this organization, as most business doctrine now implicitly agrees, that the success of the modern business enterprise now depends. Were this organization dismembered or otherwise lost, there is no certainty that it could be put together again. To enlarge it to undertake new tasks is an expensive and sometimes uncertain undertaking. Here one now finds the problem of an uncertainly high supply price at the margin. And here one finds the accompanying power. Our next task is to examine in some depth this new locus of power in the business enterprise and in the society.

*   *   *

The individual has far more standing in our culture than the group. An individual has a presumption of accomplishment; a committee has a presumption of inaction. We react sympathetically to the individual who seeks to safeguard his personality from engulfment by the mass. We call for proof, at least in principle, before curbing his aggressions against society. Individuals have souls; corporations are notably soulless. The entrepreneur—individualistic, restless, with vision, guile and courage—has been the economists' only hero. The great business organization arouses no similar admiration. Admission to heaven is individually and by families; the top management even of an enterprise with an excellent corporate image cannot yet go in as a group. To have, in pursuit of truth, to assert the superiority of the organization over the individual for important social tasks is a taxing prospect.

Yet it is a necessary task. It is not to individuals but to organizations that power in the business enterprise and power in the society has passed. And modern economic society can only be understood as an effort, wholly successful, to synthesize by organization a group personality far superior *for its purposes* to a natural person and with the added advantage of immortality.

The need for such a group personality begins with the circumstance that in modern industry a large number of decisions, and *all* that are important, draw on information possessed by more than one man. Typically they draw on the specialized scientific and technical knowledge, the accumulated information or experience and the artistic or intuitive sense of many persons. And this is guided by further information which is assembled, analyzed and interpreted by professionals using highly technical equipment. The final decision will be informed only as it draws systematically on all those whose information is relevant. Nor, human beings what they are, can it take all of the information that is offered at face value. There must, additionally, be a mechanism for testing each person's contribution for its relevance and reliability as it is brought to bear on the decision.

The need to draw on, and appraise, the information of numerous individuals in modern industrial decision-making has three principal points of origin. It derives, first, from the technological requirements of modern industry. It is not that these are always inordinately sophisticated; a man of moderate genius could, quite conceivably, provide himself with the knowledge of the various branches of metallurgy and chemistry, and of engineering, procurement, production management, quality control, labor relations, styling and merchandising which are involved in the development of a modern motor car. But even moderate genius is in unpredictable supply, and to keep abreast of all these branches of science, engineering and art would be time-consuming even for a genius. The elementary solution, which allows of the use of far more common talent and with far greater predictability of result, is to have men who are appropriately qualified or experienced in each limited area of specialized knowledge or art. Their information is then combined for carrying out the design and production of the vehicle. It is a common public impression, not discouraged by scientists, engineers and industrialists, that modern scientific, engineering and industrial achievements are the work of a new and quite remarkable race of men. This is pure vanity; were it so, there would be few such achievements. The real accomplishment of modern science and technology consists in taking ordinary men, informing them narrowly and deeply and then, through appropriate organization, arranging to have their knowledge combined with that of other specialized but equally ordinary men. This dispenses with the need for genius. The resulting performance, though less inspiring, is far more predictable.

The second factor requiring the combination of specialized talent derives from advanced technology, the associated use of capital, and the resulting need for planning with its accompanying control of environment. The market is, in remarkable degree, an intellectually undemanding institution. The Wisconsin farmer, aforementioned, need not anticipate his requirements for fertilizers, pesticides or even machine parts; the market stocks and supplies them. The cost of these is substantially the same for the man of intelligence and for his neighbor who, under medical examination, shows daylight in either ear. And the farmer need have no price or selling strategy; the market takes all his milk at the ruling price. Much of the appeal of the market, to economists at least, has been from the way it seems to simplify life. Better orderly error than complex truth.

For complexity enters with planning and is endemic thereto. The manufacturer of missiles, space vehicles or modern aircraft must foresee the requirements for specialized plant, specialized manpower, exotic materials and intricate components and take steps to insure their availability when they are needed. For procuring such things, we have seen, the market is either unreliable or unavailable. And there is no open market for the finished product. Everything here depends on the care and skill with which contracts are sought and nurtured in Washington or in Whitehall or Paris.

The same foresight and responding action are required, in lesser degree, from manufacturers of automobiles, processed foods and detergents. They too must foresee requirements and manage markets. Planning, in short, requires a great variety of information. It requires variously informed men and men who are suitably specialized in obtaining the requisite information. There must be men whose knowledge allows them to foresee need and to insure a supply of labor, materials and other production requirements; those who have knowledge to plan price strategies and see that customers are suitably persuaded to buy at these prices; those who, at higher levels of technology, are so informed that they can work effectively with the state to see that it is suitably guided; and those who can organize the flow of information that the above tasks and many others require. Thus, to the requirements of technology for specialized technical and scientific talent are added the very large further requirements of the planning that technology makes necessary.

Finally, following from the need for this variety of specialized talent, is the need for its coordination. Talent must be brought to bear on the common purpose. More specifically, on large and small matters, information must be extracted from the various specialists, tested for its reliability and relevance, and made to yield a decision. This process, which is much misunderstood, requires a special word.

The modern business organization, or that part which has to do with guidance and direction, consists of numerous individuals who are engaged, at any given time, in obtaining, digesting or exchanging and testing information. A very large part of the exchange and testing of information is by word-of-mouth—a discussion in an office, at lunch or over the telephone. But the most typical procedure is through the committee and the committee meeting. One can do worse than think of a business organization as a hierarchy of committees. Coordination, in turn, consists in assigning the appropriate talent to committees, intervening on occasion to force a decision, and, as the case may be, announcing the decision or carrying it as information for a yet further decision by a yet higher committee.

Nor should it be supposed that this is an inefficient procedure. On the contrary it is, normally, the only efficient procedure. Association in a committee enables each member to come to know the intellectual resources and the reliability of his colleagues. Committee discussion enables members to pool information under circumstances which allow, also, of immediate probing to assess the relevance and reliability of the information offered. Uncertainty about one's information or error is revealed as in no other way. There is also, no doubt, considerable stimulus to mental effort from such association. One may enjoy the luxury of torpor in private but not so comfortably in public at least during working hours. Men who believe themselves deeply engaged in private thought are usually doing nothing. Committees are condemned by the cliché that individual effort is somehow superior to group effort; by those who guiltily suspect that since group effort is more congenial, it must be less productive; and by those who do not see that the process of extracting, and especially of testing, information has necessarily a somewhat undirected quality—briskly conducted meetings invariably decide matters previously decided; and by those who fail to realize that highly paid men, when sitting around a table as a committee, are not necessarily wasting more time than, in the aggregate, they would each waste in private by themselves. Forthright and determined administrators frequently react to belief in the superior capacity of individuals for decision by abolishing all committees. They then constitute working parties, task forces, assault teams or executive groups in order to avoid the one truly disastrous consequence of their action which would be that they should make the decisions themselves.

Thus decision in the modern business enterprise is the product not of individuals but of groups. The groups are numerous, as often informal as formal, and subject to constant change in composition. Each contains the men possessed of the information, or with access to the information, that bears on the particular decision together with those whose skill consists in extracting and testing this information and obtaining a conclusion. This is how men act successfully on matters where no single one, however exalted or intelligent, has more than a fraction of the necessary knowledge. It is what makes modern business possible, and in other contexts it is what makes modern government possible. It is fortunate that men of limited knowledge are so constituted that they can work together in this way. Were it otherwise, business and government, at any given moment, would be at a standstill awaiting the appearance of a man with the requisite breadth of knowledge to resolve the problem presently at hand. Some further characteristics of group decision-making must now be noticed.

Group decision-making extends deeply into the business enterprise. Effective participation is not closely related to rank in the formal hierarchy of the organization. This takes an effort of mind to grasp. Everyone is influenced by the stereotyped organization chart of the business enterprise. At its top is the Board of Directors and the Board Chairman; next comes the President; next comes the Executive Vice President; thereafter come the Department or Divisional heads —those who preside over the Chevrolet division, the large-generators division, the computer division. Power is assumed to pass down from the pinnacle. Those at the top give orders; those below relay them on or respond.

This happens, but only in very simple organizations—the peacetime drill of the National Guard or a troop of Boy Scouts moving out on Saturday maneuvers. Elsewhere the decision will require information. Some power will then pass to the person or persons who have this information. If this knowledge is highly particular to themselves then their power becomes very great. In Los Alamos, during the development of the atomic bomb, Enrico Fermi rode a bicycle up the hill to work; Major General Leslie R. Groves presided in grandeur over the entire Manhattan District. Fermi had the final word on numerous questions of feasibility and design. In association with a handful of others he could, at various early stages, have brought the entire enterprise to an end. No such power resided with Groves. At any moment he could have been replaced without loss and with possible benefit.

When power is exercised by a group, not only does it pass into the organization but it passes irrevocably. If an individual has taken a decision he can be called before another individual, who is his superior in the hierarchy, his information can be examined and his decision reversed by the greater wisdom or experience of the superior. But if the decision required the combined information of a group, it cannot be safely reversed by an individual. He will have to get the judgment of other specialists. This returns the power once more to organization.

No one should insist, in these matters, on pure cases. There will often be instances when an individual has the knowledge to modify or change the finding of a group. But the broad rule holds: If a decision requires the specialized knowledge of a group of men, it is subject to safe review only by the similar knowledge of a similar group. Group decision, unless acted upon by another group, tends to be absolute.

Next, it must not be supposed that group decision is important only in such evident instances as nuclear technology or space mechanics. Simple products are made and packaged by sophisticated processes. And the most massive programs of market control, together with the most specialized marketing talent, are used on behalf of soap, detergents, cigarettes, aspirin, packaged cereals and gasoline. These, beyond others, are the valued advertising accounts. The simplicity and uniformity of these products require the investment of compensatingly elaborate science and art to suppress market influences and make prices and amounts sold subject to the largest possible measure of control. For these products too, decision passes to a group which combines specialized and esoteric knowledge. Here too power goes deeply and more or less irrevocably into the organization.

For purposes of pedagogy, I have sometimes illustrated these tendencies by reference to a technically uncomplicated product, which, unaccountably, neither General Electric nor Westinghouse has yet placed on the market. It is a toaster of standard performance, the pop-up kind, except that it etches on the surface of the toast, in darker carbon, one of a selection of standard messages or designs. For the elegant, an attractive monogram would be available or a coat of arms; for the devout, at breakfast there would be an appropriate devotional message from the Reverend Billy Graham; for the patriotic or worried, there would be an aphorism urging vigilance from Mr. J. Edgar Hoover; for modern painters and economists, there would be a purely abstract design. A restaurant version would sell advertising or urge the peaceful integration of public eating places.

Conceivably this is a vision that could come from the head of General Electric. But the systematic proliferation of such ideas is the designated function of much more lowly men who are charged with product development. At an early stage in the development of the toaster the participation of specialists in engineering, production, styling and design and possibly philosophy, art and spelling would have to be sought. No one in position to authorize the product would do so without a judgment on how the problems of inscription were to be solved and at what cost. Nor, ordinarily, would an adverse finding on technical and economic feasibility be overridden. At some stage, further development would become contingent on the findings of market researchers and merchandise experts on whether the toaster could be sold and at what price. Nor would an adverse de-

cision by this group be overruled. In the end there would be a comprehensive finding on the feasibility of the innovation. If unfavorable this would not be overruled. Nor, given the notoriety that attaches to lost opportunity, would be the more plausible contingency of a favorable recommendation. It will be evident that nearly all powers—initiation, character of development, rejection or acceptance—are exercised deep in the company. It is not the managers who decide. Effective power of decision is lodged deeply in the technical, planning and other specialized staff.

We must notice next that this exercise of group power can be rendered unreliable or ineffective by external interference. Not only does power pass into the organization but the quality of decision can easily be impaired by efforts of an individual to retain control over the decision-making process.

Specifically the group reaches decision by receiving and evaluating the specialized information of its members. If it is to act responsibly, it must be accorded responsibility. It cannot be arbitrarily or capriciously overruled. If it is, it will develop the same tendencies to irresponsibility as an individual similarly treated.

But the tendency will be far more damaging. The efficiency of the group and the quality of its decisions depend on the quality of the information provided and the precision with which it is tested. The last increases greatly as men work together. It comes to be known that some are reliable and that some though useful are at a tacit discount. All information offered must be so weighed. The sudden intervention of a superior introduces information, often of dubious quality, that is not subject to this testing. His reliability, as a newcomer, is unknown; his information, since he is boss, may be automatically exempt from the proper discount; or his intervention may take the form of an instruction and thus be outside the process of group decision in a matter where only group decision incorporating the required specialized judgments is reliable. In all cases the intrusion is damaging.

It follows both from the tendency for

decision-making to pass down into organization and the need to protect the autonomy of the group that those who hold high formal rank in an organization —the President of General Motors or General Electric—exercise only modest powers of substantive decision. This does not mean that they are without power. This power is certainly less than conventional obeisance, professional public relations or, on occasion, personal vanity insist. Decision and ratification are often confused. The first is important; the second is not. Routine decisions, if they involve a good deal of money, are also invariably thought important. The nominal head of a large corporation, though with slight power, and, perhaps, in the first stages of retirement, is visible, tangible and comprehensible. It is tempting and perhaps valuable for the corporate personality to attribute to him power of decision that, in fact, belongs to a dull and not easily comprehended collectivity. Nor is it a valid explanation that the boss, though impotent on specific questions, acts on broad issues of policy. Such issues of policy, if genuine, are preeminently the ones that require the specialized information of the group.

Leadership does cast the membership of the groups that make the decisions and it constitutes and reconstitutes these groups in accordance with changing need. This is its most important function. In an economy where organized intelligence is the decisive factor of production this is not unimportant. On the contrary. But it cannot be supposed that it can replace or even second-guess organized intelligence on substantive decisions.

In the past, leadership in business organization was identified with the entrepreneur—the individual who united ownership or control of capital with capacity for organizing the other factors of production and, in most contexts, with a further capacity for innovation. With the rise of the modern corporation, the emergence of the organization required by modern technology and planning and the divorce of the owner of the capital from control of the enterprise, the entrepreneur no longer exists as an individual person in the mature industrial enterprise. Everyday discourse, except in the economics textbooks, recognizes this change. It replaces the entrepreneur, as the directing force of the enterprise, with management. This is a collective and imperfectly defined entity; in the large corporation it embraces chairman, president, those vice presidents with important staff or departmental responsibility, occupants of other major staff positions and, perhaps, division or department heads not included above. It includes, however, only a small proportion of those who, as participants, contribute information to group decisions. This latter group is very large; it extends from the most senior officials of the corporation to where it meets, at the outer perimeter, the white and blue collar workers whose function is to conform more or less mechanically to instruction or routine. It embraces all who bring specialized knowledge, talent or experience to group decision-making. This, not the management, is the guiding intelligence—the brain—of the enterprise. There is no name for all who participate in group decision-making or the organization which they form. I propose to call this organization the Technostructure.

Theodore J. Lowi

A NEW FRAMEWORK FOR THE STUDY OF POWER

The apparent failure of case studies to produce hypotheses relatable to general theories of political behavior prompted Theodore J. Lowi, political scientist at the University of Chicago, to propose a new framework for investigating the nature of power and policy-making. In these excerpts from a lengthy review article, Lowi identifies three major categories of public policy, each characterized by a unique political structure.

CASE-STUDIES of the policy-making process constitute one of the more important methods of political science analysis. Beginning with Schattschneider, Herring, and others in the 1930's, case-studies have been conducted on a great variety of decisions. They have varied in subject-matter and format, in scope and rigor, but they form a distinguishable body of literature which continues to grow year by year. The most recent addition, a book-length study by Raymond Bauer and his associates, stands with Robert A. Dahl's prize-winning *Who Governs?* (New Haven 1961) as the best yet to appear. With its publication a new level of sophistication has been reached. The standards of research its authors have set will indeed be difficult to uphold in the future. *American Business and Public Policy* is an analysis of political relationships within the context of a single, well-defined issue—foreign trade. It is an analysis of business attitudes, strategies, communications and, through these, business relationships in politics. The analysis makes use of the best behavioral research techniques without losing sight of the rich context of policies, traditions, and institutions. Thus, it does not, in Dahl's words, exchange relevance for rigor; rather it is standing proof that the two—relevance and rigor—are not mutually exclusive goals.

But what do all the case-studies, including *American Business and Public Policy*, add up to? As a result of these case materials, how much farther along the road of political theory are we? What questions have the authors of these studies raised, and what non-obvious hypotheses and generalizations about "who rules and why" would we have lacked without them? Because of what it does, what it implies and what it does not do, *American Business and Public Policy* provides a proper occasion for asking these questions and for attempting once again to formulate theories that will convert the discrete facts of the case-studies into elements that can be assessed, weighed, and cumulated. But, first, what theories have we now, and how does this significant new study relate to them?

EXISTING NOTIONS: THE NON-THEORIES OF POWER IN AMERICA

It was inevitable that some general notions about power and public policy would develop out of the case-study literature. Together, these notions form what is variously called the group theory, the pressure-group, or the pluralist model of the democratic political system (a model recently also applied to non-democratic systems). No theory or approach has ever come closer to defining and unifying the field of political science than pluralism, perhaps because it fitted so nicely both the outlook of revered Federalist #10 and the observables of the New Deal. Group theory provided a rationale for the weakness of parties and the electoral process. It provided an appropriate defense for the particular programs pursued by the New Deal and

From "American Business, Public Policy, Case Studies and Political Theory," by Theodore J. Lowi, *World Politics*, XVI (July, 1964), 677–682, 687–703, 709–715 [Complete text, 677–715]. Reprinted by permission of Theodore J. Lowi and the Center of International Studies, Princeton University.

successive Administrations. And, more importantly, it seemed to provide an instant explanation, in more or less generalizable terms, of the politics of each decision. Analysis requires simply an inventory of the group participants and their strategies, usually in chronological form—for, after all, politics is a process. Each group participant is a datum, and power is attributed in terms of inferred patterns of advantage and indulgence in the final decision. The extremists have treated government ("formal institutions") as a *tabula rasa,* with policy as the residue of the "interplay of forces" measurable as a "parallelogram." More sophisticated analysts avoided the government-as-blank-key approach by treating officials as simply other units in the group process, where Congressman and bureaucrat were brokers but with their own interests and resources.

In group theory, all resources are treated as equivalent and interchangeable. And all the varieties of interaction among groups and between groups and officials are also treated as equivalent, to such an extent that only one term is employed for all forms of political interaction: the *coalition.* Coalitions, so the argument goes, form around "shared attitudes" and are extended by expansion of the stakes of the controversy. Two types of strategies comprise the dynamics of the process: internal and external. The first refers to the problem of cohesion in the midst of overlapping memberships; cohesion is a determinant of full use of group resources. The second refers to expansion of the coalition and the strategy of its use. Large coalitions beat small coalitions. System equilibrium (of unquestionably high-priority value to pluralists) is maintained by the requirement of majority-size coalitions, which are extremely difficult to create but which must be created virtually from scratch for each issue. Thus, power is highly decentralized, fluid, and situational. There is no single elite, but a "multicentered" system in which the centers exist in a conflict-and-bargaining relation to each other.

As an argument that the group must be the major unit of analysis, plural-

ism excites little controversy. But controversy is unavoidable insofar as the pluralist model implies a theory of power or power distribution. Most importantly, the pluralist model has, until recently, failed to take into account the general economic *and* political structure within which the group process takes place. On this basis, the leading type of critique of the pluralist model is a set of explicit propositions about power structure and elites. The typical answer to pluralism is a straightforward Marxian assumption that there is a one-for-one relation between socio-economic status and power over public decisions. Perhaps the more sophisticated version is a combination Marx-Weber approach which specifies the particular status bases most closely related to power—i.e., the major "orders" of society (*ständen*) in our day are the military, the industrial, and the political hierarchies.

This is no place to enter into an elaborate critique of either of these approaches or of the pluralist approach itself. Suffice it to say that while the pluralist model has failed to take the abiding, institutional factors sufficiently into account, the "social stratification" and "power elite" schools wrongly assume a simple relation between status and power. Both these latter schools mistake the resources of power for power itself, and escape analytic and empirical problems by the route of definition. There is no denying, however, that the social-stratification or power-elite approaches can explain *certain* important outcomes in a more intuitively satisfactory manner than the pluralist model precisely because each emphasizes that, while coalition-forming may be universal, not all coalitions are equivalent. For certain types of issues (without accepting Mills's argument that these are all the "key" issues), it seems clear that decisions are made by high public and private "officials" in virtually a public opinion and interest-group opinion vacuum. One does not have to go all the way with Mills and insist that behind all apparent conflict there is an elite whose members all agree on specific major policy goals as well as long-range aims. But the pluralist is equally unwise who refuses to recognize that "command post" positions in all orders of society are highly legitimate, and that the recruitment and grooming of these institutional leaders make possible a reduction in the number of basic conflicts among them, and equally possible (1) many stable and abiding agreements on policy, (2) accommodation to conflict by more formal, hierarchical means ("through channels") than coalition politics, and (3) settlement of conflict by more informal means (i.e., among gentlemen, without debates and votes) that maintain the leaders' legitimacy and stability.

There is still a third approach to power and policy-making, no less important than the others, which has not been self-consciously employed since its creation in 1935 because it was mistakenly taken as a case of pluralism. I refer to E. E. Schattschneider's conclusions in *Politics, Pressures and the Tariff* (New York 1935). Schattschneider observed a multiplicity of groups in a decentralized and bargaining arena, but the nature of relations among participants was not in the strictest sense pluralistic. The pluralist model stresses conflict and conflict resolution through bargaining among groups and coalitions organized around shared interests. The elitists stress conflict *reduction* among formal officeholders in a much more restricted, centralized, and stable arena. What Schattschneider saw was neither, but contained elements of both. His political arena was decentralized and multi-centered, but relationships among participants were based upon "mutual non-interference" among uncommon interests. The "power structure" was stabilized toward the "command posts" (in this case, the House Ways and Means Committee), not because the officials were above pressure groups, but because the pattern of access led to supportive relations between pressure groups and officials. What may appear to one observer as evidence of a power elite appears to another as decentralized pluralism (to such an extent, indeed, that Schattschneider is often credited with an important share in the founding of pluralist political analysis). Schatt-

schneider's masterful case-study actually reveals neither. At one point he concludes: "A policy that is so hospitable and catholic as the protective tariff disorganizes the opposition."[1] In many important cases completely unrelated to the tariff and much more recent than 1930, we can find plenty of evidence to support this third or fourth approach to a "theory" of power and policy-making. But as a general theory Schattschneider's conclusions would be no more satisfactory than any one approach identified earlier.

The main trouble with all these approaches is that they do not generate related propositions that can be tested by research and experience. Moreover, the findings of studies based upon any one of them are not cumulative. Finally, in the absence of logical relations between the "theory" and the propositions, the "theory" becomes self-directing and self-supportive. This is why I have employed the term "theory" only with grave reservations and quotation marks.

The pluralist approach has generated case-study after case-study that "proves" the model with findings directed by the approach itself. Issues are chosen for research because conflict made them public; group influence is found because in public conflict groups participate whether they are influential or not. Group influence can be attributed because groups so often share in the *definition* of the issue and have taken positions that are more or less directly congruent with the outcomes. An indulged group was influential, and a deprived group was uninfluential; but that leaves no room for group *irrelevancy*.

The elitist approach is no less without a means of self-assessment. If power distributions are defined as "inherently hierarchical," then a case of coalition politics either represents non-exhaustive research or concerns an issue that is not fundamental and so only involves the "middle levels of power." One need not look for theoretical weaknesses in Schattschneider's approach because his inter-

---

[1] E. E. Schattschneider, *Politics, Pressures and the Tariff*, 88.

pretation was mistakenly thrown in with the pluralists. This is most unfortunate, because if the differences between Schatt-schneider's discoveries (especially his insights into a different *type* of coalition) and those of later case writers had been recognized, a more sophisticated kind of ordered pluralism might have resulted. This is coming close to the approach I will presently propose.

* * *

It seems to me that the reason for lack of interesting and non-obvious generalization from cases and other specific empirical studies is clearly that the broad-gauged theories of politics are not related, perhaps are not relatable, to observable cases. In general, American political science seems to be subject to a continuing fission of theory and research, in which the empiricist is not sufficiently mindful of his role as system-builder and the system-builder is not sufficiently mindful (if at all) of the role that theory is supposed to play. What is needed is a basis for cumulating, comparing, and contrasting diverse findings. Such a framework or interpretative scheme would bring the diverse cases and findings into a more consistent relation to each other and would begin to suggest generalizations sufficiently close to the data to be relevant and sufficiently abstract to be subject to more broadly theoretical treatment.

An attempt at such a framework follows. For over two years prior to the publication of *American Business and Public Policy* I had been working on a general interpretative scheme. The hypotheses drawn from the scheme have so far anticipated most of the patterns described in existing case literature, and few of those patterns not anticipated have been found to be inconsistent with a logical extension of the scheme. A review article as the first published use of the scheme for national politics seemed appropriate because Bauer, Pool, and Dexter's case-study is the most elaborate case yet published, and it appeared long after most of my hypotheses had been developed.

The scheme is based upon the following argument: (1) The types of relationships to be found among people are determined by their expectations—by what they hope to achieve or get from relating to others. (2) In politics, expectations are determined by governmental outputs or policies. (3) Therefore, a political relationship is determined by the type of policy at stake, so that for every type of policy there is likely to be a distinctive type of political relationship. If power is defined as a share in the making of policy, or authoritative allocations, then the political relationship in question is a power relationship or, over time, a power structure. As Dahl would say, one must ask, "Power for *what?*" One must control for the *scope* of power and look for elites, power structures, and the like within each of the predefined scopes or "issue areas." My analysis moves in this direction, but farther. Issues as such are too ephemeral; it is on the basis of established expectations and a history of earlier government decisions *of the same type* that single issues are fought out. The study of single issues provides a good test of hypotheses about structure, but the hypotheses must be arrived at in some other, independent way.

Obviously, the major analytic problem is that of identifying types of outputs or policies. The approach I have taken is to define policies in terms of their impact or expected impact on the society. When policies are defined this way, there are only a limited number of types; when all is said and done, there are only a limited number of functions that governments can perform. This approach cashiers the "politics of agriculture" and the "politics of education" or, even more narrowly but typically, "the politics of the ARA bill" or "the politics of the 1956 Aid to Education bill," in which the composition and strategy of the participants are fairly well-known before the study is begun. But it maintains the pluralist's resistance to the assumption that there is only one power structure for every political system. My approach replaces the descriptive, subject-matter categories of the pluralists with functional categories. There is no need to argue that the classification scheme exhausts all the possibilities even among domestic policies; it is sufficient if most policies and the agencies that implement them can be categorized with little, if any, damage to the nuances.

There are three major categories of public policies in the scheme: distribution, regulation, and redistribution. These types are historically as well as functionally distinct, distribution being almost the exclusive type of national domestic policy from 1789 until virtually 1890. Agitation for regulatory and redistributive policies began at about the same time, but regulation had become an established fact before any headway at all was made in redistribution.

These categories are not mere contrivances for purposes of simplification. They are meant to correspond to real phenomena—so much so that the major hypotheses of the scheme follow directly from the categories and their definitions. Thus, *these areas of policy or government activity constitute real arenas of power*. Each arena tends to develop its own characteristic political structure, political process, elites, and group relations. What remains is to identify these arenas, to formulate hypotheses about the attributes of each, and to test the scheme by how many empirical relationships it can anticipate and explain.

AREAS OF POLICY DEFINED

(1) In the long run, all governmental policies may be considered redistributive, because in the long run some people pay in taxes more than they receive in services. Or, all may be thought regulatory because, in the long run, a governmental decision on the use of resources can only displace a private decision about the same resource or at least reduce private alternatives about the resource. But politics works in the short run, and in the short run certain kinds of government decisions can be made without regard to limited resources. Policies of this kind are called "distributive," a term first coined for nineteenth-century land policies, but easily extended to include most contemporary public land and resource policies; rivers and harbors ("pork barrel") programs; defense procurement and R & D; labor, business, and agricultural "clientele" services; and the traditional tariff. Distributive policies are characterized by the ease with which they can be disaggregated and dispensed unit by small unit, each unit more or less in isolation from other units and from any general rule. "Patronage" in the fullest meaning of the word can be taken as a synonym for "distributive." These are policies that are virtually not policies at all but are highly individualized decisions that only by accumulation can be called a policy. They are policies in which the indulged and the deprived, the loser and the recipient, need never come into direct confrontation. Indeed, in many instances of distributive policy, the deprived cannot as a class be identified, because the most influential among them can be accommodated by further disaggregation of the stakes.

(2) Regulatory policies are also specific and individual in their impact, but they are not capable of the almost infinite amount of disaggregation typical of distributive policies. Although the laws are stated in general terms ("Arrange the transportation system artistically." "Thou shalt not show favoritism in pricing."), the impact of regulatory decisions is clearly one of directly raising costs and/ or reducing or expanding the alternatives of private individuals ("Get off the grass!" "Produce kosher if you advertise kosher!"). Regulatory policies are distinguishable from distributive in that in the short run the regulatory decision involves a direct choice as to who will be indulged and who deprived. Not all applicants for a single television channel or an overseas air route can be propitiated. Enforcement of an unfair labor practice on the part of management weakens management in its dealings with labor. So, while implementation is firm-by-firm and case-by-case, policies cannot be disaggregated to the level of the individual or the single firm (as in distribution), because individual decisions must be made by application of a general rule and therefore become interrelated within the broader standards of law. Decisions cumulate among all indi-

viduals affected by the law in roughly
the same way. Since the most stable lines
of perceived common impact are the
basic sectors of the economy, regulatory
decisions are cumulative largely along
sectoral lines; regulatory policies are
usually disaggregable only down to the
sector level.

(3) Redistributive policies are like
regulatory policies in the sense that relations among broad categories of private
individuals are involved and, hence, individual decisions must be interrelated.
But on all other counts there are great
differences in the nature of impact. The
categories of impact are much broader,
approaching social classes. They are,
crudely speaking, haves and have-nots,
bigness and smallness, bourgeoisie and
proletariat. The aim involved is not use
of property but property itself, not equal
treatment but equal possession, not behavior but being. The fact that our income tax is in reality only mildly redistributive does not alter the fact of the
aims and the stakes involved in income
tax policies. The same goes for our various "welfare state" programs, which are
redistributive only for those who entered
retirement or unemployment rolls without having contributed at all. The nature
of a redistributive issue is not determined by the outcome of a battle over
how redistributive a policy is going to be.
Expectations about what it *can* be, what
it threatens to be, are determinative.

ARENAS OF POWER

Once one posits the general tendency
of these areas of policy or governmental
activity to develop characteristic political
structures, a number of hypotheses become compelling. And when the various
hypotheses are accumulated, the general contours of each of the three arenas
begin quickly to resemble, respectively,
the three "general" theories of political
process identified earlier. The arena that
develops around distributive policies is
best characterized in the terms of Schattschneider's findings. The regulatory
arena corresponds to the pluralist school,
and the school's general notions are
found to be limited pretty much to this
one arena. The redistributive arena most

closely approximates, with some adapta-
tion, an elitist view of the political process. . . .

When a billion-dollar issue can be disaggregated into many millions of nickel-
dime items and each item can be dealt
with without regard to the others, multiplication of interests and of access is inevitable, and so is reduction of conflict.
All of this has the greatest of bearing on
the relations among participants and,
therefore, the "power structure." Indeed,
coalitions must be built to pass legislation and "make policy," but what of the
nature and basis of the coalitions? In
the distributive arena, political relationships approximate what Schattschneider
called "mutual non-interference"—"a
mutuality under which it is proper for
each to seek duties [indulgences] for
himself but improper and unfair to oppose duties [indulgences] sought by
others."[2] In the area of rivers and harbors, references are made to "pork barrel" and "log-rolling," but these collo-
quialisms have not been taken sufficiently
seriously. A log-rolling coalition is not
one forged of conflict, compromise, and
tangential interest but, on the contrary,
one composed of members who have absolutely nothing in common; and this is
possible because the "pork barrel" is a
container for unrelated items. This is the
typical form of relationship in the distributive arena.

The structure of these log-rolling relationships leads typically, though not always, to Congress; and the structure is
relatively stable because all who have access of any sort usually support whoever
are the leaders. And there tend to be
"elites" of a peculiar sort in the Congressional committees whose jurisdictions include the subject-matter in question.
Until recently, for instance, on tariff
matters the House Ways and Means
Committee was virtually the government.
Much the same can be said for Public
Works on rivers and harbors. It is a
broker leadership, but "policy" is best
understood as cooptation rather than
conflict and compromise.

Bauer, Pool, and Dexter are astonished

[2] *Ibid.*, 135–136.

to discover trade associations and other groups suffering from lack of funds and support. They see as paradoxical the fact that "protectionism" as a policy could win out time after time even when a majority of businessmen and Congressmen seemed on principle to favor freer trade. (There are instances of this running clear back to the 1890's.) They see as purposive Congress's "giving up" tariff-making because the "power to dole out favors is not worth the price of having to beat off and placate the insistent pleas of petitioners."[3] Astonishment and the detection of paradox and a "Congressional group mind" are evidences of an insufficiently broad point of view. There are good and theoretically interesting reasons for each of these phenomena. Distributive issues individualize conflict and provide the basis for highly stable coalitions that are virtually irrelevant to the larger policy outcomes; thousands of obscure decisions are merely accumulated into a "policy" of protection or of natural-resources development or of defense subcontracting. And Congress did not "give up" the tariff; as the tariff became a matter of regulation, . . . committee elites lost their power to contain the participants because obscure decisions became interrelated, therefore less obscure, and more controversy became built in and unavoidable.

. . . The regulatory arena could hardly be better identified than in the thousands of pages written for the whole polity by the pluralists. But, unfortunately, some translation is necessary to accommodate pluralism to its more limited universe. The regulatory arena appears to be composed of a multiplicity of groups organized around tangential relations or David Truman's "shared attitudes." Within this narrower context of regulatory decisions, one can even go so far as to accept the most extreme pluralist statement that policy tends to be a residue of the interplay of group conflict. This statement can be severely criticized only by use of examples drawn from non-regulatory decisions.

As I argued before, there is no way for regulatory policies to be disaggregated into very large numbers of unrelated items. Because individual regulatory decisions involve direct confrontations of indulged and deprived, the typical political coalition is born of conflict and compromise among tangential interests that usually involve a total sector of the economy. Thus, while the typical basis for coalition in distributive politics is uncommon interests (log-rolling), an entirely different basis is typical in regulatory politics. The pluralist went wrong only in assuming the regulatory type of coalition is *the* coalition.

One of the most significant differences between the pluralists and Bauer, Pool, and Dexter—the treatment of the phenomenon and effects of overlapping membership—becomes consistent and supportive within this scheme. In fact, it helps to clarify the distinctions I am trying to draw here. Truman, for instance, stresses overlapping membership as a source of conflict, the function of overlapping membership as the reduction of cohesion in any given group. In contrast, Bauer, Pool, and Dexter found that in tariff politics this very overlapping of membership was a condition for cohesion: ". . . unanimity (or cohesion) is maintained by the use of multiple group memberships for purposes that might produce conflict within a single given group."[4] They observed that overlapping is a form of specialization allowing individual firms, or special constituent groups within larger associations, the freedom to pursue outside the association the goals that are contrary to other associated groups. Meanwhile the cohesion of the larger group is preserved for the goals that all the constituent groups share. The fact appears to be that both positions are correct. Owing to the unrelatedness of issues in distributive politics, the activities of single participants need not be related but rather can be specialized as the situation warrants it. But the relatedness of regulatory issues, at least up to the sector level of the trade association, leads to the containment of

[3] *American Business and Public Policy: The Politics of Foreign Trade*, Bauer, Pool, and Dexter, 37.

[4] *Ibid.*, 332.

all these within the association and, therefore, to the dynamic situation ascribed erroneously by Truman to all intergroup relations in all issues. When all the stakes are contained in one organization, constituents have no alternative but to fight against each other to shape the policies of that organization or actually to abandon it.

What this suggests is that the typical power structure in regulatory politics is far less stable than that in the distributive arena. Since coalitions form around shared interests, the coalitions will shift as the interests change or as conflicts of interest emerge. With such group-based and shifting patterns of conflict built into every regulatory issue, it is in most cases impossible for a Congressional committee, an administrative agency, a peak association governing board, or a social elite to contain all the participants long enough to establish a stable power elite. Policy outcomes seem inevitably to be the residue remaining after all the reductions of demands by all participants have been made in order to extend support to majority size. But a majority-sized coalition of shared interests on one issue could not possibly be entirely appropriate for some other issue. In regulatory decision-making, relationships among group leadership elements and between them on any one or more points of governmental access are too unstable to form a single policy-making elite. As a consequence, decision-making tends to pass from administrative agencies and Congressional committees to Congress, the place where uncertainties in the policy process have always been settled. Congress as an institution is the last resort for breakdowns in bargaining over policy, just as in the case of parties the primary is a last resort for breakdowns in bargaining over nominations. No one leadership group can contain the conflict by an almost infinite subdivision and distribution of the stakes. In the regulatory political process, Congress and the "balance of power" seem to play the classic role attributed to them by the pluralists, attacked as a theory by C. Wright Mills, and at least seriously questioned by Bauer, Pool, and Dexter.

The most interesting thing about the work of Bauer, Pool, and Dexter, from the standpoint of my scheme, is that they studied a policy that was undergoing a transition from distribution to regulation. It is, I feel, for this reason that they find some support for the pressure-group model but not enough to convince them of its utility. But it is this very transition that makes their case-study so interesting. Beginning with reciprocity in the 1930's, the tariff began to lose its capacity for infinite disaggregation because it slowly underwent redefinition, moving away from its purely domestic significance towards that of an instrument of international politics. In brief, the tariff, especially following World War II and our assumption of peacetime international leadership, became a means of regulating the domestic economy for international purposes. The significant feature here is not the international but the regulatory part of the redefinition. As the process of redefinition took place, a number of significant shifts in power relations took place as well, because it was no longer possible to deal with each dutiable item in isolation. Everything in Bauer, Pool, and Dexter points toward the expansion of relationships to the level of the sector. The political problem of the South was the concentration of textile industry there. Coal, oil, and rails came closer and closer to coalition. The final shift came with the 1962 Trade Expansion Act, which enabled the President for the first time to deal with broad categories (to the sector) rather than individual commodities.

Certain elements of distributive politics remain, for two obvious reasons. First, there are always efforts on the part of political leaders to disaggregate policies because this is the best way to spread the patronage and to avoid conflict. (Political actors, like economic actors, probably view open competition as a necessary evil or a last resort to be avoided at almost any cost.) Second, until 1962, the basic tariff law and schedules were still contained in the Smoot-Hawley Act. This act was amended by Reciprocal Trade but only to the extent of allowing negotiated reductions rather than reductions based on comparative costs. Until 1962, tariff politics continued to be based on commodity-by-commodity transactions, and thus until then tariff coalitions could be based upon individual firms (or even branches of large and diversified firms) and log-rolling, unrelated interests. The escape clause and peril point were maintained in the 1950's so that transactions could be made on individual items even within reciprocity. And the coalitions of strange bedfellows continued: "Offered the proper coalition, they both [New England textiles and Eastern railroads] might well have been persuaded that their interest was in the opposite direction."[5]

But despite the persistence of certain distributive features, the true nature of tariff in the 1960's emerges as regulatory policy with a developing regulatory arena. Already we can see some changes in Congress even more clearly than the few already observed in the group structure. Out of a committee (House Ways and Means) elite, we can see the emergence of Congress in a pluralist setting. Even as early as 1954–1955, the compromises eventually ratified by Congress were worked out, not in committee through direct cooptation of interests, but in the Randall Commission, a collection of the major interests in conflict. . . . Those issues that could not be thrashed out through the "group process" also could not be thrashed out in committee but had to pass on to Congress and the floor. After 1954 the battle centered on major categories of goods (even to the extent of a textile management-union entente) and the battle took place more or less openly on the floor. . . . The weakening of the Ways and Means Committee as the tariff elite is seen in the fact that in 1955 Chairman Cooper was unable to push a closed rule through. The Rules Committee, "in line with tradition," granted a closed rule but the House voted it down 207–178. . . . Bauer, Pool, and Dexter saw this as a victory for protectionism, but it is also evidence of the emerging regulatory arena—arising from the difficulty of containing conflict and

[5] *Ibid.*, 398.

policy within the governing committee. The last effort to keep the tariff as a traditional instrument of distributive politics—a motion by Reed to recommit, with instructions to write in a provision that Tariff Commission rulings under the escape clause be final except where the President finds the national security to be involved—was voted down 206–199. . . . After that, right up to 1962, it was clear that tariff decisions would not be made piecemeal. Tariff became a regulatory policy in 1962; all that remains of distributive politics now are quotas and subsidies for producers of specific commodities injured by general tariff reductions.

If Bauer, Pool, and Dexter had chosen a line of cases from the redistributive arena for their intensive analysis, most assuredly they would have found themselves in an altogether different universe, proposing different generalizations, expressing different doubts. The same would have been true of Schattschneider and of the pluralist students of regulatory cases. Compared particularly with the regulatory area, very few case-studies of redistributive decisions have ever been published. This in itself is a significant datum—which Mills attributes to the middle-level character of the issues that have gotten attention. But, whatever the reasons, it reduces the opportunities for elaborating upon and testing the scheme.

*   *   *

As the pluralists would argue, there will be a vast array of organized interests for any item on the policy agenda. But the relations among the interests and between them and government vary, and the nature of and conditions for this variation are what our political analyses should be concerned with. Let us say, in brief, that on Monday night the big associations meet in agreement and considerable cohesion on "the problem of government," the income tax, the Welfare State. On Tuesday, facing regulatory issues, the big associations break up into their constituent trade and other specialized groups, each prepared to deal with special problems in its own special ways, usually along subject-matter lines. On Wednesday night still another fission takes place as the pork barrel and the other forms of subsidy and policy patronage come under consideration. The parent groups and "catalytic groups" still exist, but by Wednesday night they have little identity. As Bauer, Pool, and Dexter would say, they have preserved their unanimity through overlapping memberships. They gain identity to the extent that they can define the issues in redistributive terms. And when interests in issues are more salient in sectoral or geographic or individual terms, the common or generalized factor will be lost in abstractness and diffuseness. This is what happened to the liberal trade groups in the tariff battles of the 1950's. . . .

Where the peak associations, led by elements of Mr. Mills's power elite, have reality, their resources and access are bound to affect power relations. Owing to their stability and the impasse (or equilibrium) in relations among broad classes of the entire society, the political structure of the redistributive arena seems to be highly stabilized, virtually institutionalized. Its stability, unlike that of the distributive arena, derives from shared interests. But in contrast to the regulatory arena, these shared interests are sufficiently stable and clear and consistent to provide the foundation for ideologies. Table A summarizes the hypothesized differences in political relationships drawn above.

Many of the other distinctive characteristics of this arena are related to, perhaps follow from, the special role of the peak associations. The cohesion of peak associations means that the special differences among related but competing groups are likely to be settled long before the policies reach the governmental agenda. In many respects the upperclass directors perform the functions in the redistributive arena that are performed by Congressional committees in the distributive arena and by committees and Congress in the regulatory arena. But the differences are crucial. In distributive policies there are as many "sides" as there are tariff items, bridges

and dams to be built, parcels of public land to be given away or leased, and so on. And there are probably as many elites as there are Congressional committees and subcommittees which have jurisdiction over distributive policies. In redistribution, there will never be more than two sides and the sides are clear, stable, and consistent. Negotiation is possible, but only for the purpose of strengthening or softening the impact of redistribution. And there is probably one elite for each side. The elites do not correspond directly to bourgeoisie and proletariat; they are better understood under Wallace Sayre's designation of "money-providing" and "service-demanding" groups. Nonetheless, the basis for coalition is broad, and it centers around those individuals most respected and best known for worth and wealth. If the top leaders did not know each other and develop common perspectives as a result of common schooling, as Mills would argue, these commonalities could easily develop later in life because the kinds of stakes involved in redistributive issues are always the same. So institutionalized does the conflict become that governmental bureaucracies themselves begin to reflect them, as do national party leaders and Administrations. Finally, just as the nature of redistributive policies influences politics towards the centralization and stabilization of conflict, so does it further influence the removal of decision-making from Congress. A decentralized and bargaining Congress can cumulate but it cannot balance, and redistributive policies require complex balancing on a very large scale. . . .

None of this suggests a power elite such as Mills would have had us believe existed, but it does suggest a type of stable and continual conflict that can only be understood in class terms. The foundation upon which the social-stratification and power-elite school rested, especially when dealing with national power, was so conceptually weak and empirically unsupported that its critics were led to err in the opposite direction by denying the direct relevance of social and institutional positions and the probability of stable decision-making elites.

TABLE A ARENAS AND POLITICAL RELATIONSHIPS: A DIAGRAMMATIC SUMMARY

Arena	Primary Political Unit	Relation Among Units	Power Structure	Stability of Structure	Primary Decisional Locus	Implementation
Distribution	Individual, firm, corporation	Log-rolling, mutual non-interference, uncommon interests	Non-conflictual elite with support groups	Stable	Congressional committee and/or agency**	Agency centralized to primary functional unit ("bureau")
Regulation*	Group	"The coalition," shared subject-matter interest, bargaining	Pluralistic, multi-centered, "theory of balance"	Unstable	Congress, in classic role	Agency decentralized from center by "delegation," mixed control
Redistribution	Association	The "peak association," class, ideology	Conflictual elite, i.e., elite and counterelite	Stable	Executive and peak associations	Agency centralized toward top (above "bureau"), elaborate standards

* Given the multiplicity of organized interests in the regulatory arena, there are obviously many cases of successful log-rolling coalitions that resemble the coalitions prevailing in distributive politics. In this respect, the difference between the regulatory and the distributive arenas is thus one of degree. The *predominant* form of coalition in regulatory politics is deemed to be that of common or tangential interest. Although the difference is only one of degree, it is significant because this prevailing type of coalition makes the regulatory arena so much more unstable, unpredictable, and non-elitist ("balance of power"). When we turn to the redistributive arena, however, we find differences of principle in every sense of the word.

** Distributive politics tends to stabilize around an institutional unit. In most cases, it is the Congressional committee (or subcommittee). But in others, particularly in the Department of Agriculture, the focus is the agency or the agency *and* the committee. In the cities, this is the arena where machine domination continues, if machines were in control in the first place.

But the relevance of that approach becomes stronger as the scope of its application is reduced and as the standards for identifying the scope are clarified. But this is equally true of the pluralist school and of those approaches based on a "politics of this-or-that policy."

To date, no study of policy can equal *American Business and Public Policy* in care, rigor, and exhaustiveness. But its very empirical superiority tends to emphasize its theoretical weaknesses. Data of given amount and quality become a richer and richer source as the context of those data is better and better understood. It is just such a context that I have attempted to sketch out here.

IV. THE MILITARY-INDUSTRIAL COMPLEX

Barry Goldwater

OUR PROTECTIVE SHIELD

The continuing hope for world peace, coupled with huge appropriations aimed at developing and stockpiling weapons, and public reaction to American armed intervention abroad, intensify accusations of control by a military-industrial complex. In the following excerpts from a speech delivered in the Senate in April 1969, Barry Goldwater, Republican of Arizona, answers the critics of a large military establishment. In addition, he blames excessive civilian controls for a number of miscalculations tending to impair national preparedness.

AS a member of the Armed Services Committee, and as a member of the Senate Preparedness Subcommittee, I am greatly interested in the growing preoccupation of some groups and individuals these days with the so-called military-industrial complex in the United States. Indeed, if I were a psychologist, I might be tempted to the conclusion that the left wing in American politics has developed a "complex over a complex."

Judging from the view expressed by many of our public officials and commentators the so-called military-industrial complex would seem to be responsible for almost all of the world's evils.

Certainly, a determined effort is underway to place at its doorstep almost full responsibility for the unfortunate war in Vietnam and the high cost of American defense.

We further find great attention being paid to the number of former military officers who have gone to work for defense-related industry. It has been shown with considerable flourish and headshaking that some 2,000 former members of the U.S. armed services in the grades of colonel and above, now are employed by companies that do business with the Defense Department. This revelation seemed to imply some kind of an unholy but nonspecific alliance on the part of industry and onetime military officers to cheat and defraud the American taxpayer....

In that connection, I should like to point out that the figure of 2,000-plus retired military officers working for defense-related industries is impressive only when it is permitted to stand by itself and without the proper explanation. These 2,000 officers are employed by 100 of the largest corporations in the world. They are employed by industries which do many billions of dollars worth of business every year. These 2,000 former military men are only a very small fraction of the tens of thousands of employees who work for these 100 industries—less than 1 percent. What is more, they represent only a small portion of the military officers who have been retired.

I am informed by the Pentagon that the number of former military officers receiving retired pay as of June 1968, totaled 232,892. I also discovered that since the end of World War II, some 36,800 officers in the highest grades,

From the *Congressional Record*, 91 Cong., 1 Sess. (April 15, 1969), 3719–3721.

colonels and above, have been retired. A total of 21,484 were retired between the years 1961 and 1968.

Mr. President, I believe these figures make it amply clear that high ranking military officers are not rushing into retirement at the beckoning of defense contractors.

Be that as it may, I believe it is long past time when these questions relating fundamentally to the defense of this Nation should be placed in their proper perspective. Let us take the military-industrial complex and examine it closely. What it amounts to is that we have a big Military Establishment, and we have a big industrial plant which helps to supply that establishment. This apparently constitutes a complex. If so, I certainly can find nothing to criticize but much to be thankful for in its existence.

Ask yourselves, for example, why we have a large, expensive Military Establishment and why we have a large and capable defense industry. The answer is simply this: We have huge worldwide responsibilities. We face tremendous worldwide challenges. In short, we urgently require both a big defense establishment and a big industrial capacity. Both are essential to our safety and to the preservation of freedom in a world fraught with totalitarian aggression.

Merely because our huge responsibilities necessitate the existence of a military-industrial complex does not automatically make that complex something we must fear or feel ashamed of.

You might consider where we would be in any negotiations which might be entered into with the Soviet Union if we did not have a big military backed by a big industrial complex to support our arguments.

You might wonder how we could possibly pretend to be interested in the freedom of smaller nations if the only military-industrial complex in the world was possessed by Communist Russia or Communist China. . . .

When the Russian sputnik went up, this Nation was deeply concerned. And that concern had to do with our inability at that time to duplicate the Soviet feat.

Now that we have the industrial capacity to equal the Russians in space or in matters related to defense, there seems to be a nationwide effort to make us feel guilty.

What would the critics of the military-industrial complex have us do? Would they have us ignore the fact that progress occurs in the field of national defense as well as in the field of social sciences? Do they want us to turn back the clock, disband our Military Establishment, and do away with our defense-related industrial capacity?

Mr. President, do these critics of what they term a military-industrial complex really want us to default on our worldwide responsibilities, turn our back on aggression and slavery, and develop a national policy of selfish isolation?

Rather than deploring the existence of a military-industrial complex, I say we should thank heavens for it. That complex gives us our protective shield. It is the bubble under which our Nation thrives and prospers. It is the armor which is unfortunately required in a world divided.

For all those who complain about the military-industrial complex, I ask this question: "What would you replace it with? Would you have the Government do it?" Well, our Government has tried it in the past, and failed—dismally so.

What is more, I believe it is fair to inquire whether the name presently applied is inclusive enough. Consider the large number of scientists who contributed all of the fundamental research necessary to develop and build nuclear weapons and other products of today's defense industries. Viewing this, should not we call it the "scientific-military-industrial complex"?

By the same token, do not forget the amount of research that has gone on in our colleges and universities in support of our defense-related projects. Maybe we should call it an "educational-scientific-military-industrial complex." Then, of course, the vast financing that goes into this effort certainly makes the economic community an integral part of any such complex. Now we have a name that runs like this: "An economic-educa-tional-scientific-military-industrial com-plex.". . .

As I have pointed out, many of the problems that are being encountered in the area of national defense today stem not so much from a military-industrial complex as they do from the mistakes and miscalculations of a "civilian com-plex" or perhaps I should say a "civilian-computer-complex." My reference here, of course, is to the Pentagon hierarchy of young civilians—often referred to as the "whiz kids"—which was erected dur-ing the McNamara era in the question-able name of "cost effectiveness." And this complex, Mr. President, was built in some measure to shut out the military voice in a large area of defense policy decisionmaking.

I suggest that the military-industrial complex is not the all-powerful structure that our liberal friends would have us believe. Certainly nobody can deny that this combination took a drubbing at the hands of Mr. McNamara and his civilian cadres during the past 8 years. . . .

If the military-industrial complex had been the irresistible giant its critics de-scribe, we would certainly today be bet-ter equipped. We would undoubtedly have a nuclear-powered Navy adequate to the challenge presented by the Soviet naval might. We would certainly have in the air—and not just on a drawing board—a manned, carry-on bomber. We would never have encountered the kind of shortages which cropped up in every area of the military as a result of the demands from Vietnam. There would have been no shortage of military heli-copters. There would have been no short-age of trained helicopter pilots. There would have been no need to use outdated and faulty equipment. No concern ever would have arisen over whether our sup-ply of bombs was sufficient to the task in Southeast Asia.

In conclusion, Mr. President, I want to point out that a very strong case can be made for the need for a more powerful military-industrial complex than we have had during the past 8 years. At the very least, I wish to say that the employ-ment practices of industries doing busi-ness with the Pentagon—practices which lead them to hire the most knowledge-able men to do their work—are no cause for shock. Nor are these practices dan-gerous to the American people.

I have great faith in the civilian lead-ers of our Government and of our mili-tary services. I have no desire to see the voice of the military become all-powerful or even dominant in our national affairs. But I do believe that the military view-point must always be heard in the high-est councils of our Government in all matters directly affecting the protection and security of our Nation.

Irving L. Horowitz

THE NEW CIVILIAN MILITARISTS

For several years, sociologist Irving L. Horowitz has exhibited an interest in the nature of power. In the selection below, he critically analyzes the assumptions and recommendations of a group of civilian intellectuals who advise both the government and the military on the strategy and tactics of war-making. Horowitz especially deplores the apparent absence of humanism in those individuals playing "value neutral" war games.

WHO are the new civilian militarists? First, they are men who make military policy without being officially connected to any branch of army, navy or air force service. Second, they are men trained in the strategy and tactics of military terrorism who, under the protection of university and government agencies, claim and proclaim their "neutrality" with respect to social and political values.

In these pages the names of many of these men appear: Herman Kahn, Thomas C. Schelling, Henry A. Kissinger, and Matthew Wohlstetter. While it is clear that they exhibit many policy differences in their thinking, a collective portrait does nonetheless emerge. They have a shared philosophy, a common approach to problems. They replace problems of principles with matters of strategy. They prefer thinking about the unthinkable at the costs of any examination of what is possible and preferable. They inhabit a world of nightmarish intellectual "play," while ridiculing the "ossification" of American military posture. They seem to prefer "advisory" positions and leave to politicians the actual tasks of acting out their recommendations (how else can they claim to be "value neutral" with respect to scientific canons). In brief, they are "military" minds with "civilian" status. Hence, I have designated them: the new civilian militarists—the real life counterparts of the devotees to "fail safe" technological politics.

It has been suggested by the more Panglossian elements in American intellectual circles that the new civilian militarists are not really taken seriously by the United States government, hence why should they be taken so seriously by those concerned with survival in a thermonuclear age. *Time: The Weekly Newsmagazine* (August 3, 1962) has punctured this naive optimism once and for all. Its description of "The Pentagon's Whiz Kids" (Alain C. Enthoven, Harold Brown, Henry S. Rowen, Martin Joseph Peck, and Adam Yarmolinsky) makes crystal clear the policy making and policy planning roles of the new civilian militarists. What emerges from the *Time* collective portrait are the following facts and figures:

(*a*) They are the principal advisors to the Department of Defense under the present Secretary, Robert McNamara.

(*b*) They have the direct "ear" of President Kennedy and other members of the Executive's "official family."

(*c*) They belong primarily to the technological sector of the American professional elite—with a preponderance of engineers, physicists, and economists.

(*d*) They have so outflanked military "tacticians" that, in the words of the article, the military "themselves are now bringing in younger, university-trained soldier-scientists to act as the military equivalent of the Whiz Kids."

(e) For the most part, the new civilian militarists received their nurturing in the training grounds of the RAND corporation—making studies of conventional and nuclear war, and studying the worth of such bulwarks of peace-making as the Strategic Air Command (SAC), Tactical Air Command (TAC) and the Air Defense Command (ADC).

The position of the new civilian militarists is aptly summed up by Marton J. Peck, when he said that: "Defense is really the dominant problem of our times." It is the burden of this work to show this to be incorrect; to show in contrast that: *Disarmament* is really the dominant problem of our times. In the crucible of this debate inheres the furies that will either consume us or preserve us.

During the last several years a great deal has happened both in the strategy and tactics of war-making, and in the technological potential for human destruction. Unfortunately, it cannot be said that advances registered by the strategists of peace during this same period have kept pace. Indeed, the disparity between military strategy for conflict and civilian strategy for cooperation seems constantly to be widening. The former becomes more precise and the latter more strident. In addition to which, not a few men of learning have been pressed into military activities. There are as yet pitifully few examples of military men adopting civilian attitudes.

Considering the statistics which continually press upon us this is readily understandable. Thermonuclear weapons that are one hundred times as devastating as those that laid ruin to Hiroshima and Nagasaki have been developed and made operational. Even cautious statisticians indicate that anywhere from one-third to one-half the populations of the United States and the Soviet Union would be annihilated in any multistrike hydrogen bomb exchange. We can only guess at the terrors of somatic and genetic dislocations that would follow in the wake of a thermonuclear explosion. These are

but a few of the consequences predicted for a Post World War III epoch.

Such information tends to blunt rather than stimulate interest in the problem of disarmament. The typical psychic reaction of a cancer patient doomed to die within a stipulated period of time is known as privatization; it takes the form of retreat from worldly concerns or of accelerated ego gratification. The same is true of social deviance in general. What we are witnessing is a form of privatization in which society knows the facts, yet feels impotent in the face of them. What must therefore be avoided is any tendentious repetition of the horrible but well-known facts; what must be emphasized is that no social analysis thus far made has demonstrated that society is in the position of a cancer patient. We have every right to assume the possibility between men and nations of a durable and valid peace.

The meshed problem of deterrence and disarmament is obviously long and broad. To discuss it in general terms would be a disservice, leading at best to soothing abstractions and sentimental aphorisms. Neither will get us out of this protracted period of privatization we are in. I shall therefore limit this section to a discussion of recent trends in arms control, and argue the thesis that arms control is not a substitute for a general disarmament policy, but its very opposite. And further, that the very substitution of one for the other in the name of *realpolitik* is another aspect of the privatization process (at the national level), subverting rather than supporting the search for peaceful alternatives to thermonuclear decimation and depopulation.

Before offering my analysis I think it only fair to present the rationale and conclusions of the new civilian military analysts of RAND, ITEK, IBM and the various Centers of International Relations. Clearly, this agonizing reappraisal has significant policy-making ramifications. It had, in part at least, its origins in the correct assumption that the new role of the Soviet Union as a thermonuclear power of at least equal strength to ourselves required a re-evaluation of the strategy and tactics of war-making no less than in the goals and consequences of foreign policy. It was in the despairing aftermath of the Sputnik launchings that most of this new thinking about our arms control was undertaken. Academic strategists in the United States, who until the Soviet thrusts into outer space were tolerated as purveyors of mathematical paradoxes, came to be respected as necessary adjutants in policy decisions. At present, the strategists of deterrence have so influenced military and political thinking on United States arms policy, that discussions that do not take this shift into account belong to whatever political-military counterpart there is to the neolithic age.

In tabular form, the recommendations of the new civilian militarists (which I shall throughout abbreviate as NCM) are as follows:

(*a*) The policy of disarmament should be made contingent upon the aims of national policy and national security. All stages in arms control therefore should be tactical representations of national self-interests. Thus, such matters as the escalation or de-escalation of the arms race, or the feasibility of disarmament negotiations, are not central principles of foreign policy, but rather strategies in deterring aggression.

(*b*) The United States and the Soviet Union are in a delicate balance of terror, which reduces itself to a bi-polar arms race. Other participant-players in the thermonuclear game tend to form partnerships or alliances with one of the sides of the pole. As of now, these "Nth players" contribute to rather than detract from the symmetry of the terror balance only because two nations hold the overwhelming majority of the blue chips—in this case thermonuclear warheads. But this terror balance is an unstable equilibrium, threatening to become more delicate and less balanced with the passage of time, for the technological reason that initial strikes and retaliations are programmed to occur in minutes and even seconds of each other, opening the possibility of mistakes in calculation. There is also the geo-political reason of the maturation of an Nth player who has independent interests.

(*c*) In the thermonuclear age an advantage accrues to the aggressor. This follows from the enormous expansion in the total destructive power of modern hydrogen weapons. According to the game theory principles of von Neumann and Morgenstern, a player can secure a gain of predictable dimensions irrespective of what the other player does or is planning to do. This situation only increases the rate and tempo of thermonuclear arms build-up and places an enormous premium on cheating, bluffing, *blitzkrieg* tactics, and "the game of chicken."

(*d*) In view of this situation, approaches to disarmament cannot lead to a serious resolution of outstanding world problems, since maintenance of the delicate balance of terror rests on assuming a relative equality of strength of the conflicting powers, an equilibrium that cannot be shown to obtain at any given moment. Thus arms control, defined as the maintenance of symmetry between conflicting players, is the only fruitful line of political discourse.

(*e*) Popular thinking, including that of most military strategists, rests on a false premise, namely, that present-day weapons if used would destroy mankind. While Herman Kahn, in particular, maintains that "doomsday" weapons can be programmed in the near future, the likelihood that this will come about is slim, given the tactical absurdity of programming self-annihilation as a means of victory. It is true that anywhere from ten to one hundred million people might perish in a hydrogen blast, but this is not total disaster. Man and his cultural institutions would probably survive even a multistrike thermonuclear war.

(*f*) Given this set of conditions, bipolar discussions ought to turn on the following hinges: how rapid a thermonuclear retaliation should be programmed, under what conditions ought we to make the first strike, how rapid would be the recovery rate from such a war, and what are the prospects for a re-establishment of social and political hegemony after a nuclear conflict? All of these questions are predicated on the assumption that a thermonuclear war, while it would represent an *unprecedented* catastrophe, would by no means be an *unlimited* one.

(g) We ought to prepare now for the eventuality of a thermonuclear war, rather than to assume its impossibility. This preparation, in addition to its clear-cut psychological advantages, allows for the development of instruments for measuring the extent of somatic damage, of area evacuation programs and of experiments in evolving chemical and biological counteragents to nuclear damage. An advantage in terms of federal policy is also involved, since victory in thermonuclear war might well be determined by that population able to recover quickest.

(h) Finally, the problems for the period following a thermonuclear conflict are the forms of survival and reconstruction, problems that do not exist in a pacifist stance that assumes that all forms of human life would perish. Advanced planning would include exploration of the kinds of conditional surrender thermonuclear and technological power makes possible, and the kinds of checks needed to prevent violation of agreements arising from a negotiated settlement.

*   *   *

That the NCM have gained such a wide hearing is more a consequence of the general breakdown in the disarmament dialogue between the great powers, than of any intrinsic merit in game theory proposals. In different ways, but with convergence at the functional level, the United States and the Soviet Union are witnessing what C. Wright Mills correctly described as the rise of the cheerful robot and the technological idiot. If war game theory has done nothing else, it has alerted us to the dangers of mathematical techniques uninformed by the logic of the social sciences, to a rationalism isolated from reason. This dualism of rationality and reason, so clearly embodied in the NCM, has several and diverse roots, perhaps the most important of which is the absolute separation of "is" questions from "ought" problems. What began as science's proud declaration of independence from any political or theological edicts has, through the mechanism of *expertise,* spilled over

into the much larger assumption that indifference to valuational issues, if not stupidity in the face of them, is the best possible pose for the true scientific mind. The NCM tend to adopt a physician's attitude toward his work: they provide policy makers with carefully sifted information, comparative analysis of data, and the likely consequences of taking or not taking the line of action indicated; what the policy makers do with such information becomes their own business.

There is surely a moral undercurrent in the method that sees the game theorist as diagnostician and society as a patient. This method has the appearance of satisfying the historical identification of science with social welfare, while preserving an emotional identification with the neutral and objective image culled from experimental physics. The task of this paper is not to explain the pathology of the NCM; to do this would require a detailed examination of their recruitment policies and practices, their educational orientations, their prestige and status strivings, and the professionalization of the area. I would like, however, to call attention to Laski's thoughtful criticism of *expertise* made several years ago.

It is one thing to urge the need for expert consultation at every stage in making policy; it is another thing, and a very different thing, to insist that the experts' judgment must be final. For special knowledge and the highly-trained mind produce their own limitations which, in the realm of statesmanship, are of decisive importance. *Expertise,* it may be argued, sacrifices the insight of common sense to intensity of experience. It breeds an inability to accept new views from the very depth of its preoccupation with its own conclusions. It too often fails to see round its subject. It sees its results out of perspective by making them the center of relevance to which all other results must be related. Too often, also, it lacks humility; and this breeds in its possessors a failure in proportion which makes them fail to see the obvious which is before their very noses. It has, also, a certain caste spirit about it, so that experts tend to neglect all evidence which does not come from those who belong to their own ranks. Above all, perhaps, and this most urgently where human problems are concerned, the expert fails to see that every judgment he makes not purely factual in nature brings with it a scheme of values which has no special validity about it. He tends to confuse the importance of his facts with the importance of what he proposes to do about them.

That the overwhelming majority of men *are* capable of seeing beyond the immediate gratification of desires into the wider consequences of a course of action is indicative of the uses of reason in relation to problems of war. Certainly, the change in scientific and industrial conditions, and the creation of powerful weapons of annihilation have served to minimize the self-interest argument for war that is at the center of NCM proposals.

Morris Janowitz

THE PROFESSIONAL SOLDIER

The high-ranking military officer plays a dominant role in the power elite hypothesis. In these excerpts from *The Professional Soldier,* sociologist Morris Janowitz doubts the validity of this assertion. Perceiving the American military establishment as a massive administrative pressure group, and therefore subject to a variety of internal conflicts, Janowitz argues that the professional soldier has tended to avoid both involvement in nonbudgetary political issues, and social integration into the civilian community.

C. W. MILLS suggests that contemporary military leaders are like corporation managers, and are even, in a sense, managers who are interchangeable among various types of organization, thus creating a power elite. There is little to be learned from a theory which can be reduced to the simple formula that a manager is a manager, regardless of his organizational environment. The organizational revolution in warfare means that the process of advancement and promotion is not merely the result of technical and combat skill, but also the result of communication, persuasion, and negotiation—and these are, to be sure, the practices of all types of organizational leaders. The professional soldier, like the corporation manager, must learn that interpersonal issues are crucial in the internal effectiveness of his organization. He must learn that the success or failure of his particular organization depends in part on representational skills in dealing with other military organizations and with civilian groups.

Yet, the purposes of military organization are profoundly different from those of business organization, and the loyalties and logic of the professional soldier in his managerial capacities are also different. Merely to state that the military elite are managers throws no light on who is recruited into the military, on how military education and a military career fashion the outlook of the professional soldier.

*   *   *

If the military style of life strives to produce an internally cohesive community, at the same time, it thwarts social integration with civilian society. Despite its increased size, and its elaborate organizational alliances with other civilian leadership groups, the military profession and its elite members are not effectively integrated, on a social basis, with other leadership groups. There is little evidence to support the argument that the military forms an integral part of a compact social group which constitutes the power elite. Rather, in fact, the contrary seems to be the case: namely, the political behavior of the military in the United States is still deeply conditioned by its social isolation. Much of the "public relations" efforts of the military have been an effort to gain social access to other, newer elites, particularly to scientific and academic circles.

The elite in the United States comprise highly diffuse social elements because of the sheer size of the nation, regional differences, ethnic and religious heterogeneity, and the rapidity of mobility into leadership positions. It is a much less integrated social grouping than, for example, "the establishment" in Great Britain, with its elaborate family ties, common education, and intimate patterns of social intercourse. There is no evidence that military leadership since 1900 has become more socially integrated with other elite groups. The broadening social composition of the officer corps, its separate educational system, the military style of life, and the growth in the size of the armed forces limit social integration of the military with older and even newer elite groups.

*   *   *

The trend toward a second career for generals and admirals when they leave active duty has developed rapidly since the end of World War II. Among the 1950 military leadership sample, 40 percent of the Army generals held post-retirement assignments which could be classified as full-time. Among the admirals, a smaller percentage took civilian employment, although many undertook part-time or local community activities.

Of officers who rise to the rank of major general or rear admiral, and higher, only a minority are employed on the basis of specific technical skill. In general, their second occupations are based on administrative, negotiating, and representational skills. Often these officers are persons who have specialized knowledge of the processes of government, and who have personal access to governmental agencies. Of 222 Army generals who held post-retirement jobs in 1954, about 40 percent had had training as engineers, doctors, lawyers, dentists, ministers, or teachers. Analysis of the jobs held by men with such training indicates that they tended to function as administrative and management personnel and not as technical specialists, although their technical background assisted them in obtaining employment.

Since retired military personnel are employed in civilian occupations on the basis of their general administrative skills, the range of employment has been wide. The personal contacts the officer has made, and the connections between the military establishment and civilian organizations—business and other—create these opportunities. Employment has most frequently been with industrial corporations, followed by government service. The range includes educational institutions; voluntary associations, especially welfare agencies, trade associations; communications and transportation corporations; finance and banking. Among the one hundred sixty major generals and above who were on active duty in the Army in 1950, nineteen held business assignments by 1959, three had major governmental posts, three served as ambassadors, eight had civil service posts of varying importance, and seven were connected with educational institutions. The movement into industry is a direct result of the Dual Compensation Act which permits the retired officer to receive his retirement pay if he is not hired by a government agency.

More than four hundred high-ranking military officers have been employed in the field of industrial enterprise and finance since the end of World War II. Less than a score of military managers have made prominent careers in industry and banking, which would place them at the center of the interlocking directorates which dominate American economic life. Floyd Hunter, in his informal list of the national leaders of the United States, cites approximately four hundred seventy-five persons from various functional groupings, but mainly from business. His list includes only four military names; in addition to President Eisenhower, they are Carl Spaatz, contributing editor of *Newsweek;* Lucius D. Clay, and James H. Doolittle. Lucius Clay is the outstanding example of a professional officer turned key industrialist. In addition to being chairman of the board and chief executive officer of the Continental Can Corporation, he holds numerous corporate assignments. He is a member of the financial policy committee of General Motors, a director of the Marine Midland Trust Corporation, the American Express Company, the Lehman Corporation, the Newmont Mining Corporation, and the Metropolitan Life Insurance Company.

Within the defense contract industries —particularly aircraft, missiles, shipbuilding, and, to a lesser extent, electronics—the presence of retired military officers is widespread and indicates a new type of interlocking directorate between industry and the military establishment. All of the major aircraft and missile companies employ retired admirals and generals in key management posts; their duties involve both internal management and liaison in Washington. In June 1959, Senator Paul Douglas made public a list of 768 former military officers of the rank of colonel, naval captain, and above who were in the employ of the 100 companies and their 153 subsidiaries which in the period from July 1, 1957 to June 30, 1958 received 74.2 percent of all military prime contract awards. Breakdown of the group indicates that 218 were generals or admirals.

* * *

Much of the political debate about military personnel in government policy positions centers on a few conspicuous cases where civilian leadership sought to make use of prestigeful military officers to deal with difficult political problems. In 1946 General George C. Marshall was sent to China as the President's special representative as a reaction to the political "crisis" which developed when Ambassador Patrick Hurley unexpectedly resigned in protest to the "pro-communist elements" in the Department of State whom he accused of sabotaging his efforts to reunite China. At a cabinet meeting, Secretary of Agriculture Clinton Anderson recommended that Marshall be sent as special ambassador, because "he believed the appointment of George Marshall would take the headlines away from Hurley's resignation. . . ."[1] President Truman proposed the appointment of General Mark Clark as ambassador to the Vatican because he thought it advisable to assign a Protestant to the post, and because he believed that a soldier in this role would be more acceptable to the Congress. But he misjudged political sentiment, and the proposal was promptly dropped. Truman also sought to deal with the political problems of internal security by nominating Admiral Chester W. Nimitz as chairman of a presidential commission on internal security and individual rights.

* * *

At the state and metropolitan levels, high-ranking personnel enter civil defense work and police-type operations, occasionally, as, for example, Lieutenant General George P. Hays, who served as a member of the New York-New Jersey Waterfront Commission, an agency for controlling racketeering in the Port of New York. As state and municipal governments search for administrative talent who will accept public service salaries, retired generals and admirals become a new source of personnel. For example, in 1959 Major General Roger James Browne became Deputy Chief Administrator of New York City at a yearly salary of $20,000, after having had an extensive career as a military manager, including service as United States planner for NATO.

Since many retired officers want to continue the public service tradition,

[1] Walter Millis, ed., *The Forrestal Diaries,* New York, 1951, 113.

they prefer to enter the field of education. Either because of their prior experience as teachers in the military service, or, more likely, because of their administrative ability, education is the third most frequent post-retirement occupation among generals and admirals, after industry and business and government service. Except for the teaching of mathematics and engineering by lower-ranking officers, appointments to both military and civilian schools tend to be concentrated in the southern states. About half the retired generals and admirals who have gone into education have become presidents or deans of military academies and military schools. In addition to the temporary tenure of General Eisenhower as president at Columbia University, the list of important military figures who have accepted university posts includes, as presidents, Lieutenant General Troy Middleton, Louisiana State University; Lieutenant General Andrew B. Bruce, University of Houston; Admiral Richard L. Connolly, Long Island University; Rear Admiral Chandler, William and Mary College; and as dean of faculties of George Washington University, Vice Admiral Oswald C. Colcough, formerly Judge Advocate General of the Navy. But, as with ambassadorships, the demand for generals and admirals as university presidents has declined and retired officers are more likely to serve as administrators in the field of education, or on engineering faculties, or to become involved in research supported by government contracts. . . .

If post-retirement employment tends to disperse the professional officer and assimilate him into civilian society, his professional associations operate in the opposite direction. They are very important in strengthening the social solidarity of the regular officer both during active duty and after retirement. The military has a long tradition of societies concerned with the professional and technical aspects of warfare and the publication of professional journals. Before the Civil War there were short-lived military associations with scientific and professional aspirations, such as the West Point Philosophical Society and the

United States Naval Lyceum. As early as 1873, the United States Naval Institute was founded by a group of officers at Annapolis in conscious parallel to the British Royal United Service Institution. The *Proceedings* of the Institute have been published continuously, with increasing focus on the political aspects of war. In 1879 Army officers organized the Military Service Institution, which, along with its journal, became extinct during World War I. In the main, the professional associations and journals in the Army were organized along specialist lines, with the United States Infantry Association and its *Infantry Journal* being the most influential until the outbreak of World War II.

After 1945, the associational life of the military officer underwent a change. Much of the technical and scientific activities were channeled into civilian societies, where military officers who had advanced training found common interests with civilians. At the same time, each of the services created or transformed one of its professional associations into a general organization, designed to present the service's point of view to the public. In response to the pressure of civilian controls, the services became aware that they could influence the legislative and executive process by influencing public opinion.

The largest and most influential of these service organizations is the Air Force Association, founded in 1946, which was organized without the traditional inhibitions of the professional association in the other services. Its membership in 1958 was estimated at 52,000 persons with 125 community organizations, and included retired Air Force officers, reservists, and regular Air Force officers on active duty. According to one news source the Air Force Association had some 300 "affiliates" in the form of industrial firms, each of which paid $350 in annual dues. Approximately forty persons were employed on its staff in the Washington, D.C. office in 1958.

Like the Navy League and the Army Association, the Air Force Association is a private organization in form, and, therefore, is not directly subject to the control of the Secretary of Defense or the Secretary of the Air Force. However, in effect, it is a semi-official organ of the Air Force. Its directorate in any year represents a balance of the various elements being mobilized by the Association. In 1958 there were six Air Force officers, including Generals James Doolittle, Carl Spaatz, George Kenney, plus representatives of the reserve officers. The president was Peter J. Schenk, a former official of General Electric and subsequently president of the Raytheon Corporation, a supplier of electronics and communications equipment for the military establishment. Civilian members were executives in the aircraft and air transport field, publicists, and lawyers; there was a wide geographical distribution and no overtones of political partisanship. The directorate contained few important financial figures or socially prominent leaders. They were mainly men linked to the aviation industry, whose reputations were confined to their own circles and were not nationally based. The "intellectual" and academic spokesman was Professor W. Barton Leach, a professor of law at Harvard University and a brigadier general in the Air Force Reserve, who served as the Air Force counsel at the congressional investigation of the Air Force-Navy rivalries concerning strategic bombing missions.

While the Air Force Association does not maintain registered lobbyists in Washington, one of its functions is to supply "information" to senators and congressmen. As one of the publications of the Association states, "AFA has the information that legislators and policymakers need. . . . They turn naturally to AFA for this help because the ideas that AFA backs have won national recognition." Its major task is to act as a public relations outlet for the concept of air power, beyond the official publicity of the Department of the Air Force. The Association publishes a lavish monthly magazine, *Air Force*, with extensive advertising from Air Force contractors. It holds a variety of meetings and conferences on Air Force problems and disseminates material for the mass media.

Because the bulk of the Air Force contract funds go into the aircraft industry, the aviation manufacturers' association, Aero Space Industries Association, with its annual budget of $1,500,000 and staff of sixty, including registered lobbyists and specialists in public relations, augments the Air Force Association. Each year the Association holds a national convention at which resolutions are passed on legislation affecting the Department of the Air Force. On March 30, 1959, General Thomas D. White, Chief of Staff of the Air Force, testified before the House Defense Appropriations Subcommittee that the Air Force had used 127 planes to fly civilians and military men to the Air Force Association convention that year at Dallas, Texas. He told the committee, "I can only say we endeavor to hold it down."[2]

The propaganda technique of the Air Force Association, as reflected by analysis of its output, is mainly concerned with "selling" the importance of air power. The basic theme is the central importance of strategic retaliatory air power, although the organization does not engage in elaborate discussion of military doctrine or politico-military matters. In particular, it does not comment on nuclear test suspension and disarmament, beyond declaring its suspicion of dealing with the Soviet Union.

*   *   *

For some professional officers, after retirement, nonpartisan pressure group politics is an inadequate expression of their domestic political interests. Yet, officers who stand for elected office are so few as to constitute almost special cases, for the barriers against their entering professional politics are immense. A lifetime in a specialized career which weakens geographic affiliations renders access to organized party politics very difficult. Professional honor has inhibited direct involvement in politics. It is typical for generals to advise one another that "the best service a retired general can perform is to turn in his tongue

[2] *The New York Times*, March 31, 1959, 7.

along with his suit and mothball his opinions."[3]

The exclusion of the military professional from organized party politics is a result of the two-way struggle between generals and politicians; historically, the military have fought against the appointment of political generals, and the politicians have been opposed to the use of military service as a device for building a public reputation that could be used in politics. Since the Civil War, the military profession has struggled to assert the necessity of an academy education and a lifetime career commitment as the basis for higher command. It has fought against politically appointed National Guard officers, and even against the use of professional politicians for top political-military assignments. Patrick Hurley, an organization Republican, whose appointment as major general was sponsored by President Franklin D. Roosevelt, was the last of the political generals. Although Hurley was not given command of troops, he performed a variety of diplomatic and political-military assignments, and in part represented Roosevelt's conscious efforts to demonstrate bipartisanship in the conduct of the war.

The decline of the political general has also been hastened by the suspicions of each political party regarding any efforts by the other to use military office as a launching platform for potential candidates. Newton D. Baker told Henry Stimson that he had removed his name from a list of officers to be sent to France because he did not want the Army to be used as a source of glory for politicians. When Major Fiorello LaGuardia was proposed as brigadier general for military government operations in Italy, not only did the military professionals object to his appointment, but Republicans were opposed to giving a Democrat such a political advantage.

While military service during war-time is a political asset, especially military service as an enlisted man, it is a rare event when an academy-trained regular officer stands for election to the House

of Representatives or the Senate, and even rarer when he succeeds in getting elected. In the 86th Congress, 1959–60, Representative Frank Kowalski, a Democrat from Bridgeport, Connecticut, was the only regular officer—a retired Army colonel—and the first in many years. Kowalski apparently was sought out and given the nomination because the Democratic Party needed a Polish name to balance its slate. One of his first actions in Congress, as a member of the newly created House Armed Services Subcommittee on Manpower, was to issue an attack on the armed services for wasting expensive manpower by using "thousands" of enlisted men as houseboys, domestic servants, and chauffeurs for senior officers. Another military figure who attracted national attention in the political arena, in his efforts to obtain the governorship of Alabama on a segregationist ticket, was Rear Admiral John Crommelin, leader of "Op. 23," the naval group which opposed the Air Force B-36 program. . . .

In England this concentration of regular officers in Parliament is not taken as a threat to democratic institutions. In fact, a careful study of British parliamentary institutions by J. F. S. Ross does not even comment on their presence. The British officer, compared to the American, is more fully integrated into the fabric of society. As a retired officer he can be active in conservative politics, and such activity is compatible with civilian supremacy.

In the United States a step between nonpartisan pressure group activities and direct entrance into the political arena is activity in voluntary associations designed to influence political opinion. Professional officers do not become centrally involved in the major veterans' associations, since these groups often have an anti-"big brass" bias. The great number of smaller associations organized for the veterans of specific military units include professional officers, but these associations are avowedly unpolitical.

The major organizational effort to mobilize the extreme right wing of the military leaders was the formation of Pro-

[3] Gen. Omar Bradley, *The New York Times,* May 7, 1957, 44.

America by Colonel Robert R. McCormick and ex-Representative Hamilton Fish of New York, after the election of President Eisenhower. Many of the figures involved—both military and civilian—had been active in the Citizens for Taft Committee, under the national chairmanship of Lieutenant General Albert C. Wedemeyer, which sought to obtain the Republican presidential nomination for Senator Robert Taft. After the failure of these efforts, the more extreme partisans organized Pro-America.

Among the central figures were five military officers, all of whom were advocates of absolutist military doctrine and "Far Easterners" or MacArthur's associates. Brigadier General Bonner Fellers, who had been General MacArthur's public relations expert in Japan, was the national chairman. Two other MacArthur subordinates were on the central policy committee—Lieutenant General George D. Stratemeyer and General James A. Van Fleet, as well as General Mark Clark and General Albert C. Wedemeyer. Among the civilian members were such political figures as Dean Clarence Manion of Notre Dame Law School, ex-Senator A. W. Hawkes, of New Jersey, and Frank E. Gannett. The political objectives of the organization included passing the Bricker amendment and the Reed-Dirksen amendment to limit congressional taxing power, safeguarding states' rights, upholding the McCarren-Walter Immigration Act, abolishing the withholding tax and guaranteeing the "right to work." For national security, these retired military professionals, most of whom had been Army officers, were committed to a program of maintaining air superiority and abolishing conscription. The ideological requirements of victory led them to a political position completely at variance with the majority of their professional associates. With the political decline of Senator McCarthy, and the reassertion of a politics of compromise within the Republican Party, Pro-America lost its prominence.

Such patriotic groups attract retired regular officers whose conservative partisanship ranges from right-wing Republican to implied criticism of the two-party system. The Coalition of Patriotic Societies of America, which claims to represent 112 patriotic associations, supplies a focal point for these activities. Its annual speakers include such men as Major General Charles A. Willoughby, former staff member for General Douglas MacArthur. At its 1959 annual Washington Seminar, the theme was developed that both former and present United States leaders have been unable to understand the communist menace and have permitted it to develop in this country.

In contrast to these forms of "right wing" political behavior, there has been a complete absence of even a mild "fellow traveling" equivalent since the end of World War II. The conservative bias of the profession and internal American politics have combined to prevent such a response. Only the unknown Brigadier General Hugh B. S. Hester, quartermaster specialist, emerged as a lone critic of the militarization of American foreign policy. In a 1957 speech before the National Lawyers' Guild program for peace, the most he could offer his audience was the statement that he believed that the Russians wanted peace just as much as Americans want peace.

In summary, as a pressure group, the military profession has a unique relation to Congress and to the President because of the vital functions it performs. Yet, in many respects it conforms to the pattern typical of other pressure groups which represent professional and occupational specialists. Its activities are highly decentralized, the services and individual officers compete among themselves. None of the three forms of civilian alliance—post-retirement employment, professional association activities, and direct participation in politics—serves to integrate the military into a unified political force. With few exceptions, post-retirement employment does not link the military professional into the older and well-established financial elite groups; most frequently, he follows in the pattern of the public servant, or the organizational specialist, or the salesman for an industry seeking to expand its government defense contracts. The direct involvement of the military in partisan politics has been too limited to be significant, except to indicate the direction of sentiment and the style of politics that frustration might produce.

The conflicting interests among the military profession are perpetuated in associational life. Each faction, as it bids for public and political support, can best be described as exercising a veto. This negative power reflects the different sources of public support; the Air Force advantage in support by industrial contractors is counterbalanced by the support of the Army's pragmatic point of view by news commentators and specialized opinion leaders; the Navy draws on its special alliances with key congressional leaders.

In the short run, the pressure group activities of the military are still very much the expression of a public position, behind which professional expertise and administrative compromise operate. In the long run, it is not the civilian alliances of the military establishment, but the new public relations of the military service which has the potentiality for threatening the system of political balance. An organ of government lobbying on its own behalf—especially one which deals with such a vital function—is difficult to contain. One danger is that the new public relations, because it reflects military estimates of international relations, might in the long run distort public discussion of national defense policy, and thereby increase rigidity in international relations. More fundamentally, the proposition that requires investigation is the extent to which the new public relations is transforming the debate on national security from one of questioning alternative policies of national self-interest to a debate based on rigid ideological claims.

Marc Pilisuk and Thomas Hayden

IS THERE A MILITARY-INDUSTRIAL COMPLEX WHICH PREVENTS PEACE?

The basic assumptions defining constraints on policy alternatives lie deeply hidden in highly pluralistic social systems. The two authors of the following selection, psychologist Marc Pilisuk and Thomas Hayden, conclude that the "core assumptions" underpinning American society prevent the United States from accommodating to peace.

THE term "military-industrial complex" is very much in the literature. If its most sinister depictions are correct, then the peace researcher who works with the hope that his research may actually improve chances for world peace is wasting his time. A research finding, like a bit of knowledge, is always double-edged in what it portends for applica- tion. The project which tells us the surest steps to peace, tells us with equal certainty the steps which must be bypassed if peace is shunned. If there exists an omnipotent elite, committed to militarism, then there is simply no basis for hope that voices for peace have gotten, or can get, an influential channel into inner policy circles. If, on the other

From "Is There A Military Industrial Complex Which Prevents Peace?: Consensus and Countervailing Power in Pluralistic Systems," by Marc Pilisuk and Thomas Hayden, *The Journal of Social Issues*, XXI (July 1965), 67–68, 70–71, 91–95, 97–99, 103–105, 109–110, 112–113 [Complete text, 67–117]. Complete text also available in *The Triple Revolution: Social Problems in Depth*, edited by Robert Perrucci and Marc Pilisuk (Boston: Little, Brown, 1968). All footnotes in the above selection have been omitted. Reprinted by permission of Marc Pilisuk and The Society for the Psychological Study of Social Issues.

hand, the pluralist thesis can be said to apply in full even to basic policy directions of preparedness for war or for peace, then some influential decision makers must be eagerly awaiting the research findings on paths to peace with intentions to press for their immediate application.

Because we agree with neither of the above positions, because we believe that most research workers in this area tend either to ignore or to over-rate the potential consequences of their work to peace, and because we feel that consideration of the conditions which dictate major directions of policy is essential for an evaluation of any contribution to peace research, we are bringing the concept of the "military-industrial complex" to both the microscope and the scalpel. The implications of this inquiry point to a research approach which does have relevance to the decision process and to the most central agencies of social change, and resistance to change, within American society.

*　　*　　*

The question, "Does there exist a military-industrial complex which prevents peace?" at first seems debatable in straightforward yes-or-no terms. Indeed, it might have been answerable in the 20's or 30's but not in the post-war period. When there is permanent intermingling and coordination among military, industrial, and governmental elites, and whenever greater war-preparedness can be justified by reference to the communist movement, it becomes a much "stickier" question. Because it is sticky, the easiest conclusion to support is that a "complex" simply does not exist as an omnipresent obstacle to policy change. Indeed, this belief has become the accepted norm for "informed" discussion of interests vested in the perpetuation of military preparedness. The next most easily supported conclusion would be that we have become trapped in the hell-fires of militarism by a sinister but concealed elite of military-industrial leaders, which through its puppets, pulls the strings on every major policy decision.

This latter theory is non-conformist, radical, and smacks too closely of classical conspiracy theory to be palatable to most scholars. Indeed, the dominant attitude (explicit or tacit) in most of the new literature is that there exists no military-industrial complex capable of preventing peace. It is claimed that the military-industrial complex operates as a sub-group within the limits of an essentially civilian society. In this view the complex is seen as making an interest-conscious equation of its own interests with those of the nation as a whole. But, it is argued, this tendency of power aggrandizement is checked by countervailing interest blocks in the society. Moreover, the "complex" is not seen as having a corrosive effect on democratic processes; even if it is conceded that military and technological expertise or well-financed public relations give the "complex" unusual privilege and visibility, this is no different, in principle, from certain other influential groups, all of which are limited by the web of constraints but comprise a pluralist society. Usually, it is added that the internal differences in the "complex" such as differences among the separate services or between the military and the industrial procurement sectors, tend to restrict further its ability to impose a policy "line" on the United States.

*　　*　　*

The tendency in social science has been to study decision-making in order to study group differences; we need to study decision-making also to understand group commonalities.

Were such studies done, our hypothesis would be that certain "core beliefs" are continuously unquestioned. One of these, undoubtedly, would be that efficacy is preferable to principle in foreign affairs. In practice, this means that violence is preferable to non-violence as a means of defense. A second is that private property is preferable to collective property. A third assumption is that the particular form of constitutional government, which is practiced within the United States is preferable to any other system of government. We refer to the preferred mode as limited parliamentary democracy, a system in which institutionalized forms of direct representation are carefully retained but with fundamental limitations placed upon the prerogatives of governing. Specifically included among the areas of limitation are many matters encroaching upon corporation property and state hegemony. While adherence to this form of government is conceivably the strongest of the domestic "core values," at least among business elites, it is probably the least strongly held of the three on the international scene. American relations with, and assistance for, authoritarian and semi-feudal regimes occurs exactly in those areas where the recipient regime is evaluated primarily upon the two former assumptions and given rather extensive leeway on the latter one.

The implications of these "core beliefs" for the social system are immense, for they justify the maintenance of our largest institutional structures: the military, the corporate economy, and a system of partisan politics which protects the concept of limited democracy. These institutions, in turn, may be seen as current agencies of the more basic social structure. We use the term "social structure" as Robert S. Lynd does as the stratification of people identified according to kinship, sex, age, division of labor, race, religion, or other factors which differentiate them in terms of role, status, access to resources, and power. According to Lynd:

This structure established durable relations that hold groups of people together for certain purposes and separate them for others. Such social structures may persist over many generations. Its continuance depends upon its ability to cope with historical changes that involve absorption of new groupings and relations of men without fundamental change in the structure of the society of a kind that involves major transfer of power.[1]

The "renewable basis of power" in America at the present time underlies those institutional orders linked in consensus

relationships: military defense of private property and parliamentary democracy. These institutional orders are not permanently secure, by definition. Their maintenance involves a continuous coping with new conditions, such as technological innovation and with the inherent instabilities of a social structure which arbitrarily classifies persons by role, status, access to resources, and power. The myriad groups composing these orders are even less secure because of their weak ability to command "coping resources," e.g., the service branches are less stable than the institution of the military, particular companies are less stable than the institutions of corporate property, political parties are less stable than the institution of parliamentary government.

In the United States there is no ruling group. Nor is there any easily discernible ruling institutional order, so meshed have the separate sources of elite power become. But there is a social structure which is organized to create and protect power centers with only partial accountability. In this definition of power we are avoiding the Weber-Mills meaning of *omnipotence* and the contrary pluralist definition of power as consistently *diffuse*. We are describing the current system as one of overall "minimal accountability" and "minimal consent." We mean that the role of democratic review, based on genuine popular consent, is made marginal and reactive. Elite groups are minimally accountable to publics and have a substantial, though by no means maximum, freedom to shape popular attitudes. The reverse of our system would be one in which democratic participation would be the orienting demand around which the social structure is organized.

Some will counter this case by saying that we are measuring "reality" against an "ideal," a technique which permits the conclusion that the social structure is undemocratic according to its distance from our utopian values. This is a convenient apology for the present system, of course. We think it possible, at least in theory, to develop measures of the undemocratic in democratic conditions,

[1] Robert S. Lynd and Helen Merrill, *Middletown*, New York, 1959.

and place given social structures along a continuum. These measures, in rough form, might include such variables as economic security, education, legal guarantees, access to information, and participatory control over systems of economy, government, and jurisprudence.

The reasons for our concern with democratic process in an article questioning the power of a purported military-industrial complex are twofold. First, just as scientific method both legitimizes and promotes change in the world of knowledge, democratic method legitimizes and promotes change in the world of social institutions. Every society, regardless of how democratic, protects its core institutions in a web of widely shared values. But if the core institutions should be dictated by the requisites of military preparedness, then restrictions on the democratic process, i.e., restrictions in either mass opinion exchange (as by voluntary or imposed news management) or in decision-making bodies (as by selection of participants in a manner guaranteeing exclusion of certain positions), then such restrictions would be critical obstacles to peace.

Second, certain elements of democratic process are inimical to features of militarily oriented society, and the absence of these elements offers one type of evidence for a military-industrial complex even in the absence of a ruling elite. Secretary of Defense Robert McNamara made the point amply clear in his testimony in 1961 before the Senate Armed Services Committee:

Why should we tell Russia that the Zeus development may not be satisfactory? What we ought to be saying is that we have the most perfect anti-ICBM system that the human mind will ever devise. Instead the public domain is already full of statements that the Zeus may not be satisfactory, that it has deficiencies. I think it is absurd to release that level of information.[2]

Under subsequent questioning McNa-

mara attempted to clarify his statement that he only wished to delude Russian, not American, citizens about U.S. might. Just how this might be done was not explained.

A long established tradition exists for "executive privilege" which permits the President to refuse to release information when, in his opinion, it would be damaging to the national interest. Under modern conditions responsibility for handling information of a strategic nature is shared among military, industrial, and executive agencies. The discretion regarding when to withhold what information must also be shared. Moreover, the existence of a perpetual danger makes the justification, "in this time of national crisis" suitable to every occasion in which secrecy must be justified. McNamara's statement cited above referred not to a crisis in Cuba or Viet Nam but rather to the perpetual state of cold war crisis. And since the decision about what is to be released and when, is subject to just such management the media became dependent upon the agencies for timely leaks and major stories. This not only adds an aura of omniscience to the agencies, but gives these same agencies the power to reward "good" journalists and punish the critical ones.

The issues involved in the question of news management involve more than the elements of control available to the President, the State Department, the Department of Defense, the Central Intelligence Agency, the Atomic Energy Commission or any of the major prime contractors of defense contracts. Outright control of news flow is probably less pervasive than voluntary acquiescence to the objectives of these prominent institutions of our society. Nobody has to tell the wire services when to release a story on the bearded dictator of our hemisphere or the purported brutality of Ho Chi Minh. A frequent model, the personified devil image of an enemy, has become a press tradition. In addition to a sizeable quantity of radio and television programming and spot time purchased directly by the Pentagon, an amount of service, valued at $6 million

[2] Military Procurement Authorization, Fiscal Year 1962. Hearings before the Committee on Armed Services, U.S. Senate, 87 Cong., 1 Sess., U.S. Govt. Printing Office: 1961.

by *Variety,* is donated annually by the networks and by public relations agencies for various military shows. . . . Again, the pluralistic shell of an independent press or broadcasting media is left hollow by the absence of a countervailing social force of any significant power.

The absence of a countervailing force for peace cannot, we have claimed, be demonstrated by an absence of conflicting interests among powerful sectors of American society. Indeed, such conflicts are ever-present examples of American pluralism. Demonstrating the absence of a discussion of the shared premises, among the most potent sectors of society, would go far in highlighting the area of forced or acquiescent consensus. But even the absence of debate could not complete the case unless we can show how the accepted premises are inconsistent with requisites of a viable peacetime social system. It is to this question: of the compatibility of the unquestioned assumptions of American society with conditions of peace, that we now turn. The "core beliefs" which we listed as unchallenged by any potent locus of institutionalized power are:
   a) Efficacy is preferable to principle in foreign affairs (thus military means are chosen over non-violent means);
   b) Private property is preferable to public property; and
   c) Limited parliamentary democracy . . . is preferable to any other system of government.
What characteristics of a continuing world system devoid of military conflict fly in the face of these assumptions?

We identify three conditions for enduring peace which clash with one or more of the core beliefs. These are: 1) the requirements for programming an orderly transition and the subsequent maintenance of a non-defense economy within a highly automated and relatively affluent society; 2) the conditions for peaceful settlement of internal disputes within underdeveloped countries and between alien nations and commercial interests; and 3) the conditions under which disparities in living standards be-

tween have and have-not nations can be handled with minimum violence.

If one pools available projections regarding the offset programs, especially regional and local offset programs, necessary to maintain economic well-being in the face of disarmament in this country, the programs will highlight two important features. One is the lag time in industrial conversion. The second is the need for coordination in the timing and spacing of programs. One cannot reinvest in new home building in an area which has just been deserted by its major industry and left a ghost town. The short-term and long-term offset values of new hospitals and educational facilities will differ in the building and the utilization stages and regional offset programs have demonstrable interregional effects. . . . Plans requiring worker mobility on a large scale will require a central bank for storing job information and a smooth system for its dissemination. Such coordination will require a degree of centralization of controls beyond the realm which our assumption regarding primacy of private property would permit.

The acceptance of complete international authority even in the area of weaponry poses certain inconsistencies with the preferred "core beliefs." Non-violent settlement of Asian-African area conflicts would be slow and ineffective in protecting American interests. The elimination, however, of military preparedness, both for projected crises and for their potential escalation, requires a faith in alternate means of resolution. The phasing of the American plan for general and complete disarmament is one which says in effect: prove that the alternatives are as efficient as our arms in protection of our interests and then we disarm. In the short term, however, the effectiveness of force always looks greater.

The state of world peace contains certain conditions imposed by the fact that people now compare themselves with persons who have more of the benefits of industrialization than they themselves. Such comparative reference groups serve to increase the demand for rapid change. While modern communications heighten the pressures imposed by such comparisons, the actual disparities revealed in comparison speak for violence. Population growth rates, often as high as three percent, promise population doubling within a single generation in countries least able to provide for their members. The absolute number of illiterates as well as the absolute number of persons starving is greater now than ever before in history. Foreign aid barely offsets the disparity between declining prices paid for the prime commodities exported by underdeveloped countries and rising prices paid for the finished products imported into these countries. . . . All schemes for tight centralized planning employed by these countries to accrue and disperse scarce capital by rational means are blocked by the unchallenged assumptions on private property and limited parliamentary democracy. A recent restatement of the principle came in the report of General Lucius Clay's committee on foreign aid. The report stated that the U.S. should not assist foreign governments "in projects establishing government owned industrial and commercial enterprises which compete with existing private endeavors." When Congressman Broomfield's amendment on foreign aid resulted in cancellation of a U.S. promise to India to build a steel mill in Bokaro, Broomfield stated the case succinctly: "The main issue is private enterprise vs. state socialism."[3] Moreover, preference for forceful solutions assures that the capital now invested in preparedness will not be allocated in a gross way to the needs of underdeveloped countries. Instead, the manifest crises periodically erupting in violence justify further the need for reliance upon military preparedness.

We agree fully with an analysis by Lowi . . . distinguishing types of decisions for which elite-like forces seem to appear and hold control (redistributive) and other types in which pluralist powers battle for their respective interests (distributive). In the latter type the pie

is large and the fights are over who gets how much. Factional strife within and among military industrial and political forces in our country are largely of this nature. In redistributive decisions, the factions coalesce, for the pie itself is threatened. We have been arguing that the transition to peace is a process of redistributive decision.

Is there, then, a military-industrial complex which prevents peace? The answer is inextricably imbedded into the mainstream of American institutions and mores. Our concept is not that American society contains a ruling military-industrial complex. Our concept is more nearly that American society *is* a military-industrial complex. It can accommodate a wide range of factional interests from those concerned with the production or utilization of a particular weapon to those enraptured with the mystique of optimal global strategies. It can accommodate those with rabid desires to advance toward the brink and into limitless intensification of the arms race. It can even accommodate those who wish either to prevent war or to limit the destructiveness of war through the gradual achievement of arms control and disarmament agreements. What it cannot accommodate is the type of radical departures needed to produce enduring peace.

The requirements of a social system geared to peace, as well as the requirements for making a transition to such a social system, share a pattern of resource distribution which is different from the one the world now has. Moreover, these requirements for peace are, in significant measure, inconsistent with constraints set by the more enduring convergencies among power structures in the United States. The same is true whether one speaks of allocation of material or of intellectual resources. Both are geared to the protection of the premises rather than to avenues of change. We are not saying that war is inevitable or that the changes cannot be made. We are saying that the American political, military, and industrial system operates with certain built-in stabilizers which resist a change in the system. If there is

[3] *The Atlantic*, September 1964, 6.

to be peace, as opposed to detente or temporary absence of war, marked changes will be needed. Whether this society can or will accommodate to such changes is a question which is fundamentally different from the questions posed by most studies conventionally grouped under the rubric of peace research. One difference which marks the question of capacity to accommodate is in the theoretical conception or model of the cold war which is assumed. And a second distinction lies in the manner in which the end product of the research may be suited to meet the social forces (as apart from the intellectual arguments) which promote long-term changes in policy.

* * *

What we have been calling the military-industrial complex is an informal and changing coalition of groups with vested psychological, moral, and material interests in the continuous development and maintenance of high levels of weaponry, in preservation of colonial markets and in military-strategic conceptions of international affairs. A survey of such a complex would probably delineate no useful boundaries except those coextensive with American society and its sphere of influence. Hence, a study of the relations of *any* group to the cold war could reveal a set of economic transactions and communication activities which give it a degree of centrality in the present consensus of power. A study of those groups with more focal positions in the power complex would reveal a particular but diverse set of institutions, each somewhat unique in internal dynamics and in the peculiarities of its participation in the cold war. The essence of such study is in differentiating among the institutions for there will certainly be varying scope and depth of commitment. Likewise, some of the institutions, and perhaps many of the key individuals, will present a picture which is psychologically, economically, and politically convertible to the needs of peace.

Convertibility has several meanings.

One useful standard will be objective economic adaptability. Can the group in question *survive* a basic policy shift? Some organized social groupings within the military services and major portions of the aerospace companies may not be viable in sustained peace. If 1,800 aircraft can service all scheduled airlines in the U.S. then 33,000 aircraft and most of all aviation production facilities belonging to the U.S. armed forces could present an overabundance crisis. . . . But some firms will be able to emerge unscathed and many more could probably survive with any of a wide range of governmental offset programs. Individual viability may differ sharply from that of the institution. A study of stock holdings of the officers and directors of the major defense contracting firms could reveal the types of diversification from defense orientation which has already been occurring.

A second view of convertibility is strongly social psychological but with economic underpinnings. It deals with the condition under which the desirability of shift might outweigh the positive incentives which provide psychological sustenance within the current system. We distinguish several types of incentives which research could reveal. *Profit*, of course, is one incentive which keeps some major defense contractors content but the number wholly satisfied in this manner may be shifting with the introduction of new cost-accounting devices and competitive bidding by the Pentagon. A related incentive is *foreign investment* requiring military security. Companies with holdings in Latin America, Africa, and the Near East may be "objectively adaptable" to even total loss of these holdings. However, some, like the petroleum companies, habituated to insecure holdings and high profits, may not be planning for, or willing to accept, any alternative to the military maintenance of "friendly" regimes in underdeveloped countries. The incentive of *governmental subsidy* for technological advance is often mentioned among benefits of defense contracts. Marketable civilian goods emerge as side-products of research in electronics, aviation, and machine components. Research could reveal both beneficiaries and the neglected firms in this area. Moreover, it is not clear whether similar incentives could operate to draw firms out of the current system through governmental research offerings in the areas of automated hospital, library, educational or traffic control facilities.

Approaching the more clearly psychological incentives we consider *ideological satisfaction*. The gamut ranges from a chauvinistic dedication to exorcise devils from Godly America to basic beliefs in the ultimate nature of untested assumptions of the social structure. It includes devotion to "hard nosed," masculine, competitive market-place theories of "rational" self-interest in international relations and rationalizations of special privileges which have been defended to the point of firm belief. Ideological commitment to the arms race is far from uniform. We believe that sensitive interview studies would reveal pockets of cynicism and even guilt. They might well reveal dedication to particularistic goals at the expense of other power centers (e.g., dedication to Air Force preeminence), thus indicating strains amidst the convergencies of military, political and industrial coalitions. Further, the particular ideologies uncovered may not be consonant with the non-military goals or values of the individuals involved. This could suggest the places in which ideological transfer might occur to civilian research objectives or to the rigorous pursuit of international police operations.

A last type of incentive is *vocational satisfaction*. We know very little of the daily gratifications from the many vocational roles tied to national security. We do not know whether the lavish parties and status through personal contacts mark a peripheral or a central attraction of elite adaptations. We do not know whether the opportunities for creative intellectual effort in technology and strategy are truly basic attractions or even whether such opportunities actually exist beyond job opportunity advertisements of the electronics, missile, and Research and Development corporations.

Such knowledge could suggest the possibilities for vocational convertibility in peace time. We do know, however, that in the wax and wane of success and influence within the military-industrial system, there are appearing with increasing frequency groups of individuals who are descending in position and who may be prone to such reactions as a) intensified efforts for maintaining status (and the status quo) within the society, b) nationalistic or extremist affiliations which identify scapegoats and maintain group cohesion without realistic bases, and c) defections from positions central to the complex and realignment with forces of change.

*   *   *

The argument could still be made that a voice of protest is good and perhaps essential but that proposals for government policy are necessarily restricted to the non-protest arena. This seems not entirely true. In the area of defense spending, for example, the cold war receives a number of "fringe benefits" which are quite above and beyond the particular piece of research or hardware being purchased. A pro-defense pressure group is subsidized at congressional levels and in the regions where contracts are at stake. The Department of Defense not only directs industry to meet its needs but manages to give industry the opportunity to help define what these needs, present and future, will be. Somewhere in the defense contracts is the money which supports the defense industries' lobbyists, their retired generals, and their "educational programs" which return dividends to the cold war. Whether or not this type of governmental sponsorship of political activity was arrived at by accident or by design, it is a good model for the anti-poverty warriors in government to follow. The effect of Defense Department fiscal policies on contract recipients has not only been in the provision of money for services rendered; it has also provided a sense of righteous, patriotic pride among the more rabid cold warriors, a rationale for their own existence which is a congruent part of the strategic rationale they have helped to create for the nation's pursuits.

*   *   *

Obviously, we have not answered our own question of whether there exists a military-industrial complex which can prevent peace. We have argued that the conditions of a stable peace will differ markedly from the conditions of temporary avoidance of war and that constellations of powerful and divergent interests coalesce on certain policies which work against social change. We have tried to show that the absence of monolithic decision power among these groups, while essentially correct, is a weak argument in the absence of a countervailing force for peace. We have attempted to prejudge—on scant and early evidence—the rise of a politically viable force with a critical stake in the decisions which move us toward peace and in the particular national and local programs which will offset the nation's defense efforts. We have hinted at the nature of social science research which could prove helpful to such a countervailing force.

SUGGESTIONS FOR ADDITIONAL READING

IN addition to the works cited in this volume, serious students can select additional reading from an extensive bibliography on the nature of power, which includes such diverse personalities as Seymour M. Lipset, V. O. Key, Paul M. Sweezy, and E. Digby Baltzell. However, before embarking on a lengthy investigation, exposure to a few of the earlier writers expounding elite hypotheses might help to establish a solid foundation, and place all studies of the power structure in proper perspective. In *The Myth of the Ruling Class: Gaetano Mosca and the Elite* (Ann Arbor, 1958), James H. Meisel analyzes the political thought of one of the first individuals to develop the concept of a ruling elite. Gaetano Mosca, *The Ruling Class* (New York, 1939), provides an original source for his views. Another important theorist, Italian economist Vilfredo Pareto, outlines his ideas on elites in *The Mind and Society* (New York, 1935). For a historical review, two studies are especially noteworthy: *Elites and Society* (London, 1964), by T. B. Bottomore, offers an excellent survey of ruling class theories extending from Mosca and Pareto to Marx and Mills; and Suzanne Keller's *Beyond The Ruling Class, Strategic Elites in Modern Society* (New York, 1963) presents a detailed review of more recent works along with a thought provoking assertion concerning the future of industrial societies.

The divergence of opinion between the power-elite school and the pluralists is perhaps best illustrated by William Kornhauser, "'Power Elite' or 'Veto Groups'?" in Seymour M. Lipset and Leo Lowenthal (eds.), *Culture and Social Change, The Work of David Riesman* (New York, 1961). Through the editorial endeavors of Irving L. Horowitz, students wishing to survey the writings of C. Wright Mills have been provided with two convenient sources: *Power, Politics, and People, The Collected Essays of C. Wright Mills* (New York, 1963); and *The New Soci-*

ology, Essays in Social Science and Social Theory in Honor of C. Wright Mills (New York, 1964). In the latter volume, ten prominent scholars evaluate "C. Wright Mills as a Social Scientist." G. William Domhoff and Hoyt B. Ballard have collected and edited the major reviews of *The Power Elite*, as well as Mills' rejoinder to his critics, in *C. Wright Mills and the Power Elite* (Boston, 1968).

Studies of the structure of power on the municipal level are numerous. For purposes of comparing assumptions, methodology, and conclusions, students would do well to select Robert A. Dahl, *Who Governs? Democracy in an American City* (New Haven, 1961); Floyd Hunter, *Community Power, A Study of Decision Makers* (Chapel Hill, 1953); and Edward C. Banfield, *Political Influence* (New York, 1961).

Those wishing to pursue the question of the concentration of corporate power should first read Adolf A. Berle, Jr. and Gardiner Means, *The Modern Corporation and Private Property* (New York, 1932), in which they contend that the separation of ownership and control has freed the manager from the narrow limitations imposed by the profit motive. The Berle-Means conclusion should certainly be compared to Victor Perlo, *The Empire of High Finance* (New York, 1957), illustrating, sometimes in graphic form, the interlocking ownership and control of American business. The extent of corporate power, and the resulting necessity of governmental regulation, has also produced differing interpretations. Economist Milton Friedman, in *Capitalism and Freedom* (Chicago, 1962), places considerable faith in the forces of a free market economy; in *American Capitalism, The Concept of Countervailing Power* (Boston, 1952), John K. Galbraith traces the tendency of the economy to generate internal controls; and Adolf A. Berle, Jr. in *The 20th Century Capitalist Revolution* (New

York, 1954) explores the development of the "corporate conscience." In addition to these three books, students should not overlook essays by Carl Kaysen, "The Corporation: How Much Power? What Scope?" in Edward S. Mason (ed.), *The Corporation in Modern Society* (Cambridge, 1960); and by Earl F. Chiet, "The New Place of Business, Why Managers Cultivate Social Responsibility," in Earl F. Chiet (ed.), *The Business Establishment* (New York, 1964).

On the military-industrial complex, the complete text of President Dwight Eisenhower's farewell address appears in the January 18, 1961, issue of *The New York Times*. Two major works tending to support the presence and danger of a large military-industrial establishment are: Victor Perlo, *Militarism and Industry* (New York, 1963), a study by a Marxist showing the extent of business profits resulting from defense contracts,

and Ralph E. Lapp, *The Weapons Culture* (New York, 1968), a warning by a former physicist with the Manhattan Project that the arms race has warped our sense of values. In *The Warfare State* (New York, 1962), author and journalist Fred J. Cook suggests that the growing economic dependence upon defense-related industries inhibits efforts to seek reasonable alternatives to conflict. As early as 1956, Louis Smith presented a damning indictment in "The Garrison State, Offspring of the Cold War," *The Nation*, 177 (December 5, 1956), 461–464. A more lenient view of the military-industrial complex can be found in a collection of essays, *Disarmament and the American Economy* (New York, 1963), edited by Emile Benoit and K. E. Boulding; and in M. J. Peck and F. M. Scherer, *The Weapons Acquisition Process* (Boston, 1962).